My Family Fabric

A Story of the Allen, Rogers,
Creighton, League, Bruton,
Gates, Smith Ancestors
and My Immediate Family

Published and Printed by:
Lifevest Publishing
4901 E. Dry Creek Rd., #170
Centennial, CO 80122
www.lifevestpublishing.com

Printed in the United States of America

I.S.B.N. 1-59879-085-4

Cover Design by
Donna Harvey and Toya Harvey

My Family Fabric

A Story of the Allen, Rogers, Creighton, League, Bruton, Gates, Smith Ancestors and My Immediate Family

by Toya Allen Harvey

CONTENTS

Foreword - Dr. Francis Sullivan

Foreword, in Appreciation

On the lawn standing before the home of Toya and Bill Harvey is a stately maple tree. It was a gift to the new Harvey family from Bill's mother. Let it be symbol of the story that Toya tells in the pages that the reader will certainly savor. The tree represents in the strong roots, the high reach and the symmetry, the grace and precision of her words. Roots and branches draw for us the family bonds of humility and love. Growth pictures the range of time of many generations in a celebration of progress and life. Sturdiness suggests the striving folk so well portrayed. There is sweet nostalgia that knits this record into a sure wholeness.

The head, heart and hand of a musician are in these pages. Let the melody linger on!

Frank Sullivan, friend, doctor
June 2005

Ancestors of Toya Barbara Allen

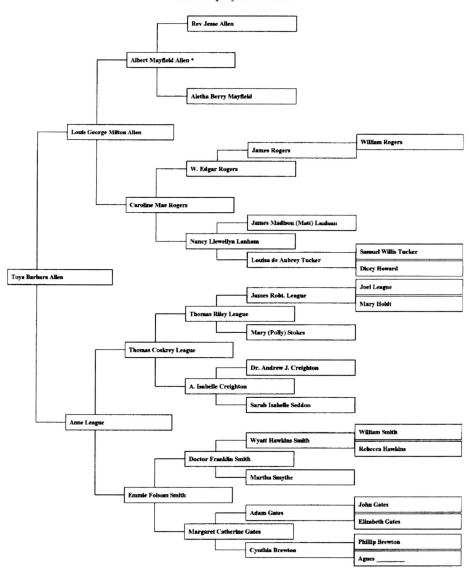

Chapter One
Ancestral Lines

My name is Toya Allen Harvey. For some years I have been writing family memories, but in 2003-2004 I began this family history. My purpose in writing this book is to give the story of my ancestors to my children, grandchildren, future generations and all who have a genealogical interest in the following family lines: Allen, League, Creighton, Gates, Brewton, Smith, Rogers, Lanham, Wofford, Tucker, Llewellyn, Putnam and Howard. Not only did I want to show the background from which our forebears came, but also to give information—information that might provide insight into the lives of our ancestors, what their personal qualities and character may have been. I have tried to present some of the conditions and deprivations our ancestors faced, particularly in the different periods of history. I am not pretending this is a 'scholarly' work but I did research some 'pieces' of history. I have attempted to weave back in time, often stumbling over obstacles of historical information. Having been able to find strands of our ancestral threads starting in Europe (as in a 'tapestry' with many patterns, designs and fabric,) I see God's handiwork evolving from a great mix of people and spreading through many centuries and cultures.

The colorful thread of Celtic culture is woven into our ancestral heritage and history has shown how the Celts contributed to our Scots-Irish ancestry. "The term Celts, historically, covers the cultures of Ireland, Scotland, Wales, Cornwall, the Isle of Man and Brittany, who were all once closely related." (D.J. Conway, The Celtic Book of Names, 1999, vii). I learned the Celtic tribes date back to the 3rd century B.C. As stated in the Eyewitness Travel Guides, Ireland (30, 1997), "The Iron Age reaches Ireland in the 3rd century B.C., *along with the Celts, who migrated from central Europe, via France and Britain, and soon established themselves as the dominant culture.*"

Who were the ancestors of the Celts? On page two of the book, <u>Who Were Those Celts?</u> Author Kevin Duffy says…"it is known with scientific certainty that the earliest , direct ancestors of the Celts lived in an area now represented by southern Germany, Austria and Switzerland."

We know the Scots and the Irish share similarities in language and history. The Scots originally came from Ireland and settled in the north of Britain. " Many of their surnames have been influenced by political allies, as well as invaders—the Roman, Vikings, Anglo-Saxons, and the French, to name a few. (Conway,p. 161).

"The Celtic language has been separated into two major branches and given the designation 'P' Celtic (as spoken in France and Wales) and 'Q' Celtic (as spoken in Ireland and Scotland…" (Duffy, p. 144.)

Since many of our people came from these areas , this adds to our understanding of who our people were and how we came to be the people we are today. Our 'League' ancestors originally came from France as French Huguenots. Our 'Gates' ancestors came from the Rhine river valley of Germany. The following statement helps to establish a relationship of our ancestors to this area: " When Louis XV expelled seven thousand Protestants from France in 1709, these Protestants known as German Palatines came from a district in southwest Germany, west of the Rhine river. Many settled in Ireland; some came to America." (Lineham, p. 46.)

French Protestants who fought for William the Conqueror, settled in Ireland and many of them were skilled artisans. (Lineham, p. 19). These French Protestants prospered in their woolen and cattle trade. Because of this, the English market was hurt and the English merchants asked Parliament for help. As a result, Ireland was forbidden to export cattle and manufactured goods. Our Irish and Scot-Irish ancestors were affected as "Restrictions were placed on their [Irish] religion; [there was] petty

2

persecution of their pastors; [and] the increase of their rents on leases expiring; and the entire destruction of their manufacturing industries [took place]..." (Lineham, p. 20). Many of our people left from Dublin, Ireland to come to America. Some like the 'Allens' were either Irish, or Scot-Irish; as well as the 'Rogers', but I believe relative, Virgil M. Rogers stated the Rogers could have been English-Irish. (Rogers-McCravy-Lanham, pp. 14-15). The 'Woffords' were probably English; the 'Llewellyns' were from Wales; but who is to say with certainty no other lines intertwined.

In speaking of the Irish, we cannot omit the resettling of Ulster, Ireland by the Scots. John C. Lineham, Irish Scots and the Scotch-Irish, discusses the resettling of people into Northern Ireland (The Plantation of Ulster 1608-1620). Ulster at this time comprised six counties which were divided into three parts: "The first was assigned to the English planters, the second to the Scotch and the third, to servitors and Irish natives (p.88).

Seven Districts: English
Nine Districts: Scotch
Nine Districts: Servitors and Irish natives

Among the names of the Irish natives is the surname, "McQuin." Since my great grandfather, Rev. Jesse Allen named his oldest son, McQueen Allen, there may be a connection between the Allen and McQueen families. On page 88 of Lineham's book, two 'McQuin' gentlemen are allotted 128 acres of land:

Hugh McQuin, gent...128 acres
Donell McQuin, gent...128 acres

Our Allen family was supposedly in Ireland until 1799 or 1800. There could have been intermarriage between the Scot and Irish branches of McQueen and Allen.

"Dobbs'History of Irish Trade (Dublin, 1727) records that three thousand males left Ulster yearly for the colonies. Philadelphia, alone for the year 1729, shows a record of 5,655 Irish emigrants, against English and Welsh, 267; Scotch 43, Germans, 343." (Lineham, quoting Dobb's 21).

An observation made by Magnus Magnussun is certainly of interest to anyone whose ancestors were Irish Protestants or Scot-Irish Protestants: "There is one fact about eighteenth-century Ireland, however, that cannot be challenged...the fact that in a largely Protestant Ulster there was so much discontent that in the second half of the century, more than a quarter of a million Ulster Presbyterians uprooted themselves and emigrated to America." (Landlord or Tenant, p. 53).

Hourglass Tree of Robert T. Rogers

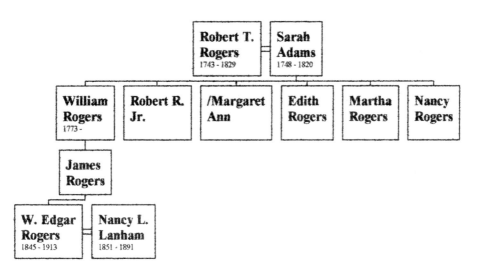

Chapter Two
Robert and Sarah Rogers

Our ancestor, Robert T. Rogers must have felt the social discontent that many others did in Ireland. He and his wife, Sarah Adams emigrated from Dublin, Ireland, and landed in Charleston, South Carolina on November 4, 1773. At that time, Robert was thirty years old.

As the ship pulled out of the harbor in Dublin, one can only wonder what Robert's thoughts were. Had it been our lot, would we question the decision to leave? Would we ask what the journey would be like and what to expect when and if we reached the 'new world'? The insecurity of 'the unknown' can certainly test a man's faith. The uncertainty of a successful crossing and their future in a new land, plus Sarah's pregnancy; all were conditions which Robert and Sarah faced.

Robert Louis Stevenson wrote: "through nine and twenty mingled years," he speaks of " what man may learn or do, of right or wrong, of false and true...

What Man May Learn, What Man May Do

What man may learn, what man may do?
of right or wrong of false or true,
While, skipper-like, his course he steers
Through nine and twenty mingled years,
Half misconceived and half forgot,
So much I know and practise not.

Old are the words of wisdom,old
The counsels of the wise and bold:
To close the ears, to check the tongue,
To keep the pining spirit young;

To act the right, to say the true,
And to be kind whate'er you do.

Thus we across the modern stage
Follow the wise of every age;
And, as oaks grow and rivers run
Unchanged in the unchanging sun,
So the eternal march of man
Goes forth on an eternal plan.
("Poetry Lovers Page Internet 4/10/02).

The day after Robert and Sarah Rogers arrived in Charleston, their son, William was born. Some time later, the Rogers family relocated to the upstate of South Carolina. Around 1785, two grants of land, 100 acres each, were received by Robert Rogers, on the Tyger River in lower Spartanburg County.

The Location of their farm on Rogers' Bridge Road is also known as Nesbitt's Bridge Road. On this land is the family cemetery where Robert T. and Sarah Rogers are buried. Photos of the burial markers and the Rogers' home place can be seen in the Rogers-McCravy-Lanham book, by Virgil M. Rogers. (21, 125-126).

According to Virgil Rogers, "The Rogers family was Scotch-Irish or English-Irish." (11). Many of the family surnames apparently entered England and Wales with the Norman invaders. The "Rogers name is found throughout Wales; the greatest numbers on the border with England."(Conway, 213).

The Rogers' line is important to our ancestry. From Robert T. Rogers to his son, William; to William's son, James; to James' son, W. Edgar—we come to my father's maternal grandmother, Nancy Llewellyn Lanham, the wife of W. Edgar Rogers. (Rogers, 123-124).

Descendants of Hugh Llewellyn

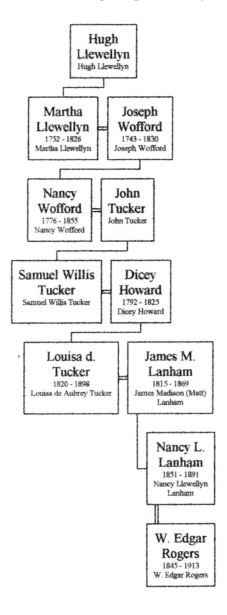

Chapter Three
Patches in our Heritage

The following information shows the lineage of my father, Louis G. Allen's maternal line from his grandmother, Nancy Llewellyn Lanham back to Hugh Llewelyn of Wales:

The name Llewelyn comes through Hugh Llewelyn, a Quaker born in Wales, who later settled in Pennsylvania, His daughter, Martha Llewelyn was born in Pennsylvania in 1752. She married Captain Joseph Wofford. He migrated in the early 1700's from the north of England to Pennsylvania near the Maryland line. After a move to Spartanburg County, South Carolina, Joseph and Martha (Llewelyn) Wofford had six children; one of whom was Nancy Wofford. She married John Tucker. John Tucker was born in England and came to America, landing in Maryland in 1768.(Rogers, Virgil. Rogers-McCravy-Lanham, 55-58).

The Welsh surnames, Llewelyn, de Aubrey, Tucker, Lanham and Wofford are part of our patchwork centered in Wales and England. Other patches in our heritage, apart from the English/ Welsh Quakers and the English puritans are important to our story,— but back to the Quaker genealogy.

Nancy Wofford and husband, John Tucker were parents of Samuel Willis Tucker. Samuel became the husband of Laodicea (Dicey) Howard, daughter of James Howard and Ruth Putnam.

James Howard was a Revolutionary soldier from Union, South Carolina (application number S 20466, found in the Revolutionary War Pension Application Record Book, Library of Congress,Genealogical Branch Center, National Archives). He served under General Nathaniel Greene's Command.

From the marriage of Samuel Willis Tucker and Dicey Howard a daughter, Louisa de Aubrey Tucker was born. Louisa de Aubrey Tucker married James Madison Lanham.

The marriage of James Madison Lanham and Louisa de Aubrey Tucker produced my great-great-grandmother, Nancy Llewellyn Lanham!! Nancy Llewellyn Lanham married W. Edgar Rogers and from this marriage, many children were born. Of great importance were two daughters, Caroline Mae Rogers and Emily Josephine Rogers. These two sisters married the same man, Dr. Albert Mayfield Allen!!

The Rogers' family and my father's mother, May Rogers (Allen) were easy-going gentle people. Was this quality inherited from our Quaker ancestor, Martha Llewellyn (Wofford)? At my father's death, (1989) Reverend Marion C. Allen, gave the grave-side eulogy. He spoke of the legacy of "gentleness" which my dad, Louis G. Allen, passed on— specifically, the "gentleness" my children and I inherited from him.

Uncle Marion especially appreciated the gentle nature of his brother because his own father (and my dad's father) was not a gentle person; rather he was a hard, demanding person. Dr. Albert Mayfield Allen may have inherited his personality traits from the dark side of the Irish/ Scots-Irish!

What do we know about our English ancestors? Perhaps they came from England with backgrounds of English and Welsh; English and Scots; English, Scots-Irish or maybe the mixture became French, German, Welsh, English and Scots-Irish? Who knows?

In the United Kingdom, the term Great Britain covers England, Wales, Scotland and Northern Ireland. These locations form the background of our 'heritage quilt.' The distinctive differences in the variety of 'patches' make our quilt more meaningful and appealing! We are drawn to the creative force that made this all possible!

The German states, protesting the revocation of Nantes, were German Protestants, later known as Lutherans. Some left Germany, as did the French Huguenots from France. These people were absorbed into Ireland, Scotland, England and America.

There were Irish and Scots who intermarried and became Scots-Irish. But there were also 'pure Scots' and 'pure Irish.' One can see the difference in a full-blooded Scotsman and a full-blooded Irishman! This difference can be seen in the Scots-Irish branches of the Allen's and Rogers'; also, the French-Scot families, the Leagues and Creightons. The Scots-Irish have fair skin, sometimes with freckles and light brown to reddish brown or reddish blonde hair. The French-Scots' complexion is not dark, but has a quality that is almost luminous, not requiring make-up for color. Our Smith line from England had medium to dark hair and lovely, clear skin—similar to that of Dutch people.

The French men were small in stature, and naturally reserved. "Papa" League was such a man—a man of few words. His sisters were all soft-spoken and mannerly. This quality changed somewhat with the union of Emmie Smith and Thomas C. League (Papa)—more on this subject when the Smith ancestry is discussed.

A form of movement, known as 'arabesque' is used in architecture, art and music. It spirals, circles, intertwines and encircles. Evergrowing and interlacing , the growth makes it difficult to determine where the movement starts and takes root! Such is the case with our British ancestors!

Chapter Four
Wagon Travelers, Regulators
and Patriots

Many ancestors traveled "the old wagon road from Philadelphia to South Carolina" or from Virginia down to South Carolina. My grandmother League spoke of her Smythe and Smith relatives coming down from Virginia. My dad, Louis G. Allen, also told of the Allen family coming down "the old wagon road." This was the route most followed after they landed in Philadelphia or Richmond. Settlers began arriving in the upstate of South Carolina as carly as 1716. (Morison, 1972, p.198.) A migration of immigrants from the British Isles, Germany and France (Internet: American History – Colonial Scots – Irish Immigrants, 25 Oct. 2003.) landed at Philadelphia and Newcastle. The Scots – Irish and Anglo-Irish who came from Ulster in Ireland were people of the "border region." (Fischer, David Hackett. Albion's Seed, selections from the Internet 25 Oct. 2003.) The Border Country (between Scotland and England) was an area that "touched upon the Irish Sea: Ayr, Dumfries and Wigtown in Scotland; Cumberland and Westmoreland in England; Derry, Antrim and Down in Ireland." (ibid.) The Irish Sea united the "surrounding lands in a single cultural region." (Ibid.)

Elizabeth Semancik created May 1, 1997: Albion's Seed Grows in the Cumberland Gap for "The American Studies Program" at the University of Virginia. She wrote of the resentment the Quakers felt for the 'audacious and disorderly' borderers from Northern Ireland. The Quaker settlement was not unhappy to see the 'rugged border people' move on to the states of Maryland, Virginia, North and South Carolina. But this movement was done 'in stages.' It was not until 1729, that North Carolina and South Carolina became "separate royal dependencies." (Kennedy, 1997, p. 23.) In the 1720's and 1730's many of the Scots-Irish settled in Pennsylvania. (American History-Scots-Irish Immigrants (Internet) originally published in The Irish At Home and Abroad journal of Irish genealogy, vol. 2 #1, 1994/1995.) As land became more expensive, the Scots-Irish and German immigrants moved on the "Great Wagon Road" path to Virginia. Some settled and stayed; others settled for a time until a need for adventure and more "bottom land" prompted them.). (Compton, Brenda E. McPherson. The Great Wagon Road, p. 5, Internet 25 Oct. 2003.) "During the first years, they walked, leading five or six pack animals laden with supplies: tools seed, fabric. In places, the famous path they trod was only three or four feet wide." Buffalo had probably worn down the path but as time went by the travelers were able to walk along side oxen pulling two-wheeled carts filled with all their 'possessions." "By 1765 the Great Wagon Road was cleared …enough to hold horse drawn vehicles and by 1775, the road stretched 700 miles." (Ibid.) "Governor Tryon of North Carolina wrote to England that more than a thousand wagons passed through Salisbury in the fall and winter of 1765… (About six immigrant wagons per day)" (Ibid.) The best mode of travel was the 'Conestoga Wagon' made by Germans in Pennsylvania. Whatever the mode, the travel was slow. The families would stop in the afternoon to care for their needs and to prepare for the night's rest. In this dangerous 'back country' one wonders if they truly could sleep! After many months of travel (supplies dwindling, bad weather conditions, and possibly a sick child or family member) the pioneers often determined to go no further. This country, known as the 'back country' was inhabited by Indian nations, the Cherokee, Creek, Choctaw and Chickasaw in the south. (http://xroads.virginia.edu/~UG97/albion/aback.cou.html)

The immigrants who entered America through the port of Charleston, SC "had progressed only about eighty or ninety miles westward." (Ramsay, History of South ,Carolina, quoted by Dr. John B.O.Landrum, in his History of Spartanburg County, Spartanburg Journal, 1954, p.9). The writer, William Gilmore Simms, The Yemassee, captured in story and poetry, the people who settled on the coast of SC…in Beaufort, SC. His story, a work of fiction, presented history, as well. The English Puritans settled in this area and lived among the Indians. Learning from each other, a treaty was observed whereby land was bought from the Indians. Gradually the Indians resented the loss of their hunting grounds; the forest— where deer, wild turkeys and bear lived. The settlers used the axe in clearing the forest to make canoes and in building log homes— and here and there— a fort, for protection from their enemies—the Yemassee. The deer hides provided clothing—moccasins, leather breeches and jackets. For sleeping and sitting, the bear skins provided comfort and warmth in the winter. The white colonials, in the area between Charleston. SC and Savannah, GA were governed by an Assembly and Governor in Charleston.

In the upstate of South Carolina (1755), the territory that became Spartanburg county had no more than "eight or ten Scotch-Irish families from Pennsylvania," who settled on the 'Forks of the Tygers.' (Landrum, 9). "Between these settlers and the settlers which had advanced from the seacoast," much land remained in the hands of the Indians. (Ibid.)

A treaty (1755) between Governor Glen of the Province of South Carolina and "Old Hop," head man of the Cherokees, granted to the Indians all the territory in present day Greenville, Anderson, Oconee and Pickens counties. The present boundaries between Greenville and Spartanburg counties and Greenville and Laurens counties are the same as the old Indian Boundary Line. A survey was completed in 1761. The treaty between "Old Hop" and South Carolina was broken when the Indians aided the British in the American Revolution. (Coleman and Givens, 1-4).

From "A Description of the Province of South Carolina "by Governor James Glen:

> The concerns of this country are so closely connected and interwoven with Indian affairs, and not only a great branch of our trade, but even the safety of this Province, do so much depend upon our continuing in friendship with the Indians, that I thought it highly necessary to gain all the knowledge I could of them...(SC Information Highway, Internet).

"The northwest section of South Carolina around Greenville and Spartanburg was the last portion of the state to be surrendered by the Cherokee Indians in 1777." (Kennedy, 85).

"This up-country region of Virginia and the Carolinas, sometimes called the 'old west,' lay so far from markets as to be almost self-sufficient..." "Huge droves of cattle were rounded up annually in Cowpens for the purpose of export to larger cities such as Charleston." (Morison, 198).

"Agriculture was the main occupation of Carolina highland settlers of the late 18th century...Farming on uncleared land meant girdling and burning trees, utilizing the natural fertility and cultivating among the trees or stumps by hoe. As the soil wore out, new ground was cultivated and the process began again." (Kennedy, 138).

The 'back-country' pioneers (1760) of South Carolina—Camden, Cheraws, the Peedee, the Wateree and the Congaree—differed greatly in "origin and religion" from the people of the 'seaboard.' These people were separated from coastal South Carolina by a "belt of pine barrens." (Morison, 263-264). This 'lawless' part of South Carolina had no courts or sheriffs. The provincial government and assembly were at Charleston, SC. "A man had to own 500 acres and 20 slaves to qualify for membership in the assembly. (Ibid.) The lack of government prompted the people to form "associations known as 'regulators' to refuse payment of taxes" until they received some type of representation. (Ibid.)

The coastal plantation owners "talked liberty, self-government, equitable taxation...within their own ruling class," but were hardly concerned with the plight of back-country settlers. Lacking any help from Charleston, the 'regulators' took matters into their own hands. (Jones, 1971, 91).

Author Richard Maxwell Brown says: "Soon the Regulators were supervising morals and family life, collecting debts, attacking the labor shortage, and finally, to assure the safety of their regime, sealing off the region from Low country interference. Acting like a government, but without authority, they soon encountered local hostility." (The SC Regulator, 83).

For a year or two, the Regulators were popular "because of their services in breaking up outlaw gangs" but excessive "disciplining of the more 'shiftless and irksome'of the lower people" resulted in a lack of support. (Brown, 89) "...the Moderator movement...brought the Regulator [in SC] to an end in the spring of 1769." (84).

Regulators were in North Carolina as early as 1763. Unlike South Carolina Regulators, the North Carolina Regulators had "courts and sheriffs, but wished to reform and regulate them..." (39-40). the government of North Carolina suppressed the NC Regulators in the Battle of Alamance (1771)—a battle in which much blood was shed. (95).

Ancestor Samuel Bruton's name is included on the North Carolina Roster of Regulators. A list of the Roster is on the Internet entitled, "Signatories to the North Carolina Regulators." A larger heading is: Captain Benjamin Merrell and the Regulators of Colonial North Carolina. (http://www.tamu.edu/ccbn/ddewitt/mckst-merindivid.htm).

The Regulator Movement backfired—but the strong feeling of independence—especially among the Scots-Irish—and their willingness to take risks for their beliefs— was evidenced when the War for Independence—the Revolutionary War took place (1776).

Despite outward circumstances and appearances, the prelude to 1776 was heard by men in South Carolina as they broke away from the Proprietors (1719) placed over them by the English and in 1770, "they divorced the king himself." (Jones, Lewis P., South Carolina, A Synoptic History for Laymen, 1971,, 90-91).

From The Oxford History of the American People vol., (1972):

By 1763, a compromise was reached between imperial control and self government...apart from minor discontents over judges and currency, Americans were satisfied with this compromise...But the government of George III was not...Hence the Revenue Act of 1764 and the Stamp Act of 1765. (Morison, 247).

"Almost everything England did or did not do about her colonies until about the year 1774 can be referred to trading considerations. It was essentially a commercial empire. The general theory...was [the] colonies existed for the benefit of the homeland." (188).

A colonial office and a colonial secretary were established in the British government until 1768. "All colonial business went through a committee of crown appointees, called the Board of Trade and Plantations." Although the colonies were not represented on this board, "almost every colony kept a salaried agent in London to defend its interests..." (190).

While grievances were taking place in Boston, Massachusetts and Charleston, South Carolina, the people of Spartanburg District, S.C. were busy building log cabins, chopping wood, planting wheat and corn and *warding off Indian attacks!* These brave pioneering families deserve honor and recognition for their spirit and courage!! When there were only a few families, "eight or ten Scotch-Irish families" (Landrum, History of Spartanburg County, 9) they relied on each other as they made soap and candles, did the cooking, milking; they washed and scrubbed the clothes, churned the milk for butter and helped in planting and tending the crops. The men built fences, wagons, hauled water, hunted for game and carried the corn and wheat to the grist mill.

Many chores were done as a group—corn shuckings, quiltings, clearing the land and building forts for protection from the Indians. Most of the settlements were near creeks because of the necessity for water.

An article (The Greenville News-Piedmont) dated 11 August 1985, gives information about the "Iron Age" in the upstate:

From the 1770's to the mid 1800's there was [an] active iron mining and iron working network in upstate South Carolina. The Old Iron District stretched from Spartanburg County east into south central North Carolina. Iron produced by the furnaces was transported by wagon to locations where it was processed into pots, pans, nails or other items. Wofford's Iron Works on Lawson's Fork Creek in Glendale near Spartanburg, was one of the first iron working sites in the upstate. It was established in 1773 and was burned down during the Revolutionary War.

As our upstate ancestors faced the challenges and hardships of raising families and providing food and shelter for them, the threat of Revolution against England was getting closer and closer. "…The American Revolution was not fought to obtain freedom, but to preserve the liberties that Americans already had as colonials." (Morison,, 296).

The emigrants came to America seeking a new life, in a new land. Their strength of character and endurance made it possible to adapt to the many trials faced by them. Their stubbornness con-tributed to their survival. As William Gilmore Simms wrote in The Yemassee:

"Thus human reason, ever confident,
Holds its own side – half-erring, half-right '
Not tutored by a sweet humility,
That else might safely steer." (vol.2, Chapter III, 18).

My paternal ancestor, Nancy Wofford (Tucker), the grand-mother of Nancy Llewellyn Lanham (Rogers) was born in Spartanburg County on June 13, 1776 and the American Revolution began July 4, 1776. The Declaration of Independence "was adopt-ed on the evening of 4 July 1776, [and] Printed copies were sent the next day to the former colonies, now states, and to the army." (Morison, 296).

In the Carolinas, civil war between the Patriots and Loyalists was most severe and prolongued. The War of Independence was a war in which the contending parties often lived side by side." (314).

Author Morison describes the colonial militia (The Oxford History of the _
American People, Vol. 1, 1972) as follows:

The colonial militia—included in theory every able-bodied man between the ages of sixteen and sixty. The sufferings of the Continental Army have not been exaggerated, but they were due to selfishness, mismanagement, and difficulties in transportation.... (302). Most American families made their own clothing at home and could not greatly increase their output...Wagon transportation was slow and costly...The need for blankets was a problem, quilts were of no use to soldiers in the field. The private soldier was badly fed, clothed, and cared for. (304).

Matthew A.C. Newsome, The Migration of the Scots-Irish to Southwestern NC tells us: "The British government did not want settlers on Cherokee land." This was not agreeable to the Scots-Irish who planned to settle there. A settlement was illegally set up in east Tennessee. "These settlers were now fighting a British enemy and a Cherokee one." During the French and Indian War, the British encouraged the Cherokees to attack the settlers. It was no surprise that the British called on the Cherokee to be an ally in the Revolution. (http://www.scottishtartans.org/ulster.html). However, Britain's "Military superiority over the thirteen colonies lay in her navy, which might have been decisive, had France not intervened." (Morison, 309).

The commander-in-chief for the Continental Army, George Washington, a capable leader of his men, "assumed every responsibility thrust upon him.." He refused to accept a salary, and used his 'modest fortune' to buy "comforts for the soldiers and to help destitute families of his companions in battle." "…Washington brought something more important to the cause than military ability and statesmanship: the priceless gift of character." (314).

Note: The majority of our ancestors traveled the "Great Wagon Road." Our North Carolina ancestor was "Regulator, Samuel Bruton," and our Patriots were John Tucker and Captain Joseph Wofford.

Descendants of Joseph Wofford

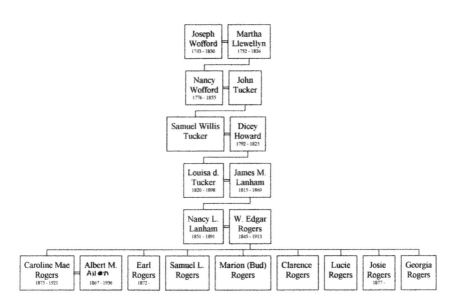

Chapter Five
Captain Joseph and Martha Wofford
and Tabernacle Methodist Church

In the early 1770's, "five brothers of this name came from Maryland, and most of them settled in the vicinity of Hill's Factory, on Tyger River."(Landrum, History of Spartanburg County, chapter XVI, 220) These 'five' descended from one of two Wofford brothers who came from the north of England and settled in Pennsylvania near the Maryland line.

One of the 'five', Joseph Wofford, was Revolutionary soldier, "...a captain of a company in the 'snow campaign,' during the winter of 1775. This company was a part of the "famous Spartan regiment under the command of Colonel John Thomas, Sr...." He was commanding the troops in Charleston, South Carolina, before the fall of that city; the troops [then] fell back to Ninety Six."(223.)

"Captain Joe" was a target for the Tories. His cabin was closely watched, in fact, he was arrested in his home by a band of Tories. The pleading of his wife (who on this night in 1780 gave birth to a son, Benjamin Wofford) resulted in his later release. This son, Benjamin, became the founder of Wofford College, Spartanburg, South Carolina.(Rogers, 56).

"Those who can justly claim Captain Joseph Wofford and his wife, Martha Llewelyn as their common ancestors, run into the thousands, and are intermingled with hundreds of families in Spartanburg County."(Landrum, 231).

Dr. John B. O. Landrum, Author of History of Spartanburg County, gives praise to the character of Capt. Joseph Wofford's wife, Martha Llewelyn, when he quotes Reverend James F. Smith, Spartanburg, SC:

"In the year 1752, there was born in Pennsylvania a daughter to Quaker parents, who, moving to Spartanburg District with that child, wrought a great influence for good in that community and ultimately for the whole district. Being brought up under the example and religious influence of that noted and worthy people, the Quakers, and educated in the best schools of the day, she was prepared to receive the Gospel from the mouths of John Mason and Thomas Davis in 1787... They believed that Gospel taught a sound conversion, 'justification by faith,' and she never rested until she attained that true and great position. Shipp's History of Methodism says: 'she traveled for fifteen years the Way to Zion alone, her husband and children not giving heed to the Teachings of the Gospel and the divine impressions that the Good Spirit Always makes, in connection with that Gospel.'

In the year 1802 however, they were awakened and converted and Brought into the Methodist Church, under the preaching of Lewis Myers And George Dougherty.

That good woman was Martha Lewellyn, the wife of Joseph Wofford, And the mother of Reverend Benjamin Wofford, the liberal founder of Wofford College, in the growing city of his native district of Spartanburg, SC. ...after living to a ripe old age in prayer and usefulness, she went to Heaven on the 24th of March 1826; leaving a gracious influence behind Her. She being dead still speaks through her children and grand and Great-grandchildren, to her church and people of her native county."(107).

Author Virgil M. Rogers relates that for approximately the first eighteen years of her married life, there was not a church available for her or her family. Her sister joined a Baptist Church but Martha was not inclined to. The Gospel preached by Methodist Missionaries, Rev. Mason and Rev. Davis, suited her spiritual needs and convictions. "She joined the Methodists and began planning for a church. Her grandson, Dr. Benjamin Wofford said it was 'largely due to her prayers and to her influence that the first humble meetinghouse was built.

In 1804 her son, Benjamin Wofford was licensed to preach (on the Methodist Circuit of the Methodist Episcopal Church.) Martha's grandson, Samuel Willis Tucker was described as 'the moving spirit and largest contributor' to the second Tabernacle Church built on the site of the first meetinghouse (1840).(Rogers, 57).

Tabernacle Methodist Church

In Tabernacle Church Cemetery are the graves of Martha Llewellyn (1752-1826) and Captain Joseph Wofford (1743-1830). The church, now known as Tabernacle United Methodist Church is "located about eight miles east of Woodruff, SC. Go Road #50 From Woodruff about one mile past I-26, turn right on Road #142. The church is about Two miles on the left and the cemetery is on the adjoining lot."("Tabernacle Tombstones," Pinckney District Chapter Newsletter, vol.10, page 7). Other ancestral families buried in the cemetery are: Louisa deAubrey Tucker (1820-1898) and James Madison Lanham (1815-1869); Nancy Wofford (1776-1855), daughter (and our line of descent) from Joseph and Martha Wofford; Laodicea Howard (1792-1825) and Samuel Willis Tucker (1792-1871).

A marker was erected at Tabernacle by the Wofford Memorial Association in Memory of the Descendants of Captain Joseph Wofford –August 8, 1902.

Readers and family, just in case you need reminders of the genealogy of the names mentioned above, please refer to chapter three, Patches in our Heritage.—- Nancy Wofford married John Tucker; their son, Samuel Willis Tucker married 'Dicey' Howard (daughter of James Howard and Ruth Putnam.) The union of Samuel Willis Tucker and Laodicea (Dicey) Putnam produced Louisa de Aubrey Tucker who married James Madison Lanham. Their child, Nancy Llewellyn Lanham married W. Edgar Rogers— my great-great-grandparents!

Descendants of Rev Jesse Allen

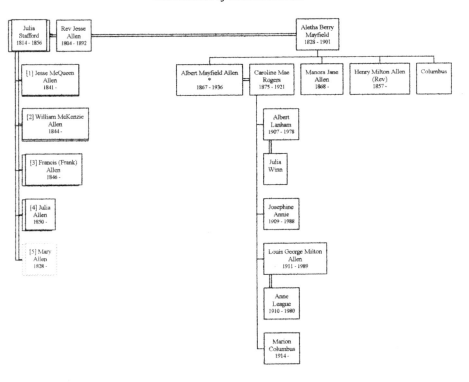

Chapter Six
Reverend Jesse Allen

The writer Coleridge once made the statement: "The mind contains clusters of facts, but it is the predominant mood of the soul that determines which of these shall be called into life, and in what pattern." As I think back on the lives of my ancestors, I wonder what was the predominant mood of the Allen's, Rogers, Leagues and the Smiths? Consider now the individual and the circumstances of the Irishman, with a 'quaint way of speaking,' Reverend Jesse Allen!

My father's paternal line dates back to his grandfather, Jesse Allen (1804-1892.) From church records, his pastorate at Liberty Hill Methodist and Abner Creek Baptist Church, we find much information. During the Civil War, he was minister at Liberty Hill. After converting to the Baptist faith in 1867, he was ordained a Baptist minister and served as pastor of Abner's Creek Baptist Church for two years—1878-79.

The dedication of a Historical Marker at Abner Creek Church was held on the 16th of September 1979. Printed Programs were provided at the ceremony. The 'Program Notes' contained "A History of Abner's Creek Church 1832-1904." Biographical information concerning Reverend Jesse was included. Not only did it speak of Jesse Allen's service as minister at Abner Creek (1878-79) but also described something of Jesse Allen, the man:

In July of the same year (1867), Rev. Jesse Allen from the Methodist Church (Liberty Hill) was received into the fellowship of the church by baptism and ordained a Baptist minister. He was an Irishman, possessed a giant mind and was a capital preacher of his day. He always attended the protracted meetings at Abner's Creek and greatly enjoyed them. He was gifted in prayer and had a voice that could be heard for a distance of more than a mile away.

He requested that he might be buried as near to the meeting house as possible. His request was carried out and a spot was selected for his grave near the north end of the old meeting house and within a few feet of the pulpit, at that time. There he is sleeping near the place that was so dear to him in his life. ....Rev. Jesse Allen was pastor in 1878 and in August a great revival meeting was held, resulting in the addition of forty seven members by experience and baptism. H.M. Allen (Jesse's son) was also ordained as a minister of the Gospel in 1878....

The obituary from the Minutes of the Spartanburg Baptist Association, 1876-1895 reported:

"Rev. Jesse Allen, a member of Abner's Creek Church, passed from earth to his eternal reward in March, 1892. He was 82 years old (this is incorrect, he was 88.) He had been in early life a minister of the Methodist persuasion and was measurably success-ful. Being of Irish extraction he carried into his work a blunt and quaint manner and delivery, but was a sensible man, and interesting preacher. He acknowledged after changing his church relations, and connecting himself with the Baptist Church, that he was never exactly happy in the performance of the ordinances as practiced by the Methodists and was ever after he came to the Baptist, as long as he lived, a cheerful man and acceptable preacher among his brethren. In his later years, he was poor in this world's goods, but his brethren at Abner's Creek opened their doors to him and con-tributed to his comfort and happiness. He died in the faith of the Gospel, in the esteem of his brethren, and no doubt, has received his crown."

This information was sent to me by Edna Henderson, Historian for Harmony Methodist Church on Highway 25, about thirty miles south of Greenville, S.C. I visited her at her home just down the road from Harmony Methodist after my husband, Bill and I had seen the graves of Julia Stafford Allen and infant daughter, in the church cemetery. Jesse married Julia Stafford in Sumter, S.C. –information from Postell Allen's research. My purpose: to verify that Jesse Allen was instrumental in the organization and founding of Harmony Methodist Church. Edna Henderson could find no mention of Jesse Allen in her church history—even so, the fact that Jesse's wife and infant daughter are buried in the church cemetery and Jesse and Julia never lived in that area provided evidence to a connection between Jesse Allen and Harmony Methodist Church! Was Jesse a "circuit rider" minister for the Methodist church?

After reading the following excerpt from a newspaper article from the Greenville News (May 1, 1994) by Rev. Bryan Crenshaw, it seemed plausible that Jesse was indeed a 'circuit rider.' In the article entitled, "Homecoming, dinner on grounds was great," the author speaks of returning to Liberty Hill United Methodist Church, "located five miles south of Greer." Rev. Crenshaw mentions "the church was organized in 1849 with 12 charter members." He continues:

In 1850 Pressley McClimon offered the group two acres of land if they would build a church and a school. This land was originally part of a land grant from the King of England to the McClimon family. A small church and school built of logs and having dirt floors was erected. It was named Liberty Hill. [The next statement supports my belief that Jesse Allen was a 'circuit rider'] The newly formed church affiliated with the Methodist Protestant Church which furnished <u>Circuit Riders </u>to visit and conduct the services.

In a letter from Edna Henderson (Oct. 17, 1997) she told me, "the Methodist Protestant Church was formed in 1830—Harmony Methodist was started in 1839 and a Mr. Arnold gave the land so that his son would have a place to preach."

From the information Postell Allen received from Jesse Allen's neighbors, Mr. McClimon and Mr. Andrew McHugh: Jesse and Julia Allen and their children moved to the 'piedmont' area of SC; first settling at Cross Anchor and later, Liberty Hill. She may have traveled with him to a 'brush arbor' meeting at Harmony

Methodist and taken ill while there. This could explain why she and the infant were buried in the church cemetery. Julia Allen's death: 10 April 1856.

Referring to Postell Allen: Jesse Allen, "upon settling near Pelham, SC began the organization of Free Methodist Protestant Churches in the nearby territory and founded among others, the following:

> Harmony Methodist, Rt. 25; 30 miles south of Greenville, SC
> Methodist church located between Easley and Greenville, SC
> Methodist church at or near Duncan, SC
> Conestee Methodist Church located at Conestee, SC

The Greenville News published an article, Wed. Aug. 28, 2002, entitled "Conestee was early center of Greenville Industry" by Judith Bainbridge: "…McBee's Chapel is the pride of Conestee, listed on the National Register of Historic Places…It is one of only three remaining octagonal churches in the U.S. and is arguably the oldest church structure in Greenville County. Supervised by mill-wright, John Adams, in its construction and completed in 1841, it seated the entire village—about 150 people—who were required to attend services by Methodist Circuit Riders."

From Georgia to South Carolina

This 'preacher-man' of strong mind and voice, whose "circuit riding" ministry led him from Sumter, South Carolina to upstate South Carolina (mainly Spartanburg County) described by those who knew him, as an "Irishman" over six feet tall and weighing over 200 pounds.

A 'story,' which may or may not be true, is that Jesse was born aboard ship coming to Richmond, Virginia from Dublin, Ireland. This information (Postell Allen's research) has a marginal note in Postell Allen's writing saying this cannot be verified. Jesse Allen's birthplace on every census is listed as the state of Virginia—1804.

Jesse in later years, "a man poor in this world's goods" (Obituary, Southern Baptist Association, 1876-1895), has a fine monument on his grave in Abner Creek Cemetery. The marker is tall and resembles a pulpit with an 'open Bible' carved into the top.

The Jesse Allen found in Sumter (1850) was a carpenter; his age, forty-five; his wife, Julianne Stafford, thirty-five. Their four children: Malissa, 10 years old; Jesse (mcQueen), 8 years old; Will (McKenzie), 6 years old; and francis, 4 years old. Deduction: Jesse was in Sumter at least ten years and married to Julia for ten years. Probably these were the years Jesse turned to the teachings of the Methodist Protestant Church.

The years before Sumter have been hard to 'piece together.' From Census and Tax Records of Fayette/Henry County, Georgia, a Jesse Allen was in Georgia during 1827-1840—"Land Lottery" years! Eligible persons were entitled to one or more draws in the Land Lottery years of 1805, 1807, 1821, 1827 and 1833. One, Jesse Allen drew 101 ¼ acres in District 13, Fayette County, GA in the year 1827. His age was twenty-three. The tax levy was .43 ¾. "A poll tax was assessed on every white male over the age of twenty-one, and the assessment for land was entered on the roll of the county in which the owner resided….and within each county, tax lists were compiled by district…" (Smoak, 'People Finders' Article, p.97).

The First Tax Digests for Fayette County, GA, 1823-1834: "May 15, 1821, the drawing for the 1821 Georgia Land Lottery was held in Milledgeville, the capitol of the state, for land in the newly created counties of Dooly, Henry, Houston, Monroe and Fayette." "Winners of this fourth Georgia Lottery began to settle in this part of Georgia, and it would be another eight years before a census of these people would be taken."

Land that was granted was taken from the Creek Indian Nation, ceded by the Creeks on January 8, 1821 to the United

States. Georgia's Governor Troop and a Special Assembly of the Legislature—May, 1821—created the five counties mentioned above.

"The new land was surveyed into nine mile square Land Districts, then subdivided into 256 land lots of 202 ½ acres each..." Jesse Allen acquired one half of a land lot.

Jesse and his Georgia family were entered on the Fayette/Henry County, GA Census for 1830 and 1840. In 1830 his age was listed as 26. The family unit included a female—age group 20-30 (his wife?)—two females under the age of five (his daughters?) and a widow, age 70-80, named Mary Allen.

There are more listings of Jesse Allen on the Tax Digests: 1829, 1833 and 1834. All have the same acreage, 101 ¼ acres; land lot 144 and District 13—and are in Fayette County, GA.

If the Jesse Allen on the Georgia Census is my great grandfather, this explains a daughter born in 1828 (remember the two females under five in 1830?) The daughter born in 1828 is shown in the family of Jesse Allen and Aletha Berry Mayfield on the 1860 Census of Woodruff/Reidville, SC.

Jesse's wife is listed as Berry, age 32 and daughter, Merry, age 32. The ages are correct, but the enumerator confused the spelling of Mary and omitted Aletha from Aletha Berry. Nevertheless, Mary is the correct spelling for Jesse's daughter from Georgia. Is she named for the widow, Mary Allen? (GA Census; 1830-1840.)

The daughter, Mary Allen married Will Rhodes, November 6, 1861 [Marriages and Death Notices from Baptist Newspapers of SC, vol.l by Brent Holcomb.] This public notice referred to Mary's father as Rev. Jesse Allen of Spartanburg County, SC.

What happened to Mary's mother and sister? And what

were their names? Did they die in Georgia? Where was Mary when Jesse was in Sumter, SC? I guess these questions will never be answered—as well as the question, "Who were the parents of Jesse Allen?"

Concerning the Tax Districts, it might be interesting to know that "Tax Districts in colonial and antebellum Georgia paralled the militia districts. They were political units, laid out originally to include the number of males best suited to the operation of a military company. A District's Tax receiver was the elected militia captain." (Georgia Militia Districts by Alex M. Hitz, pp1-4).

Descendants of Julia Stafford

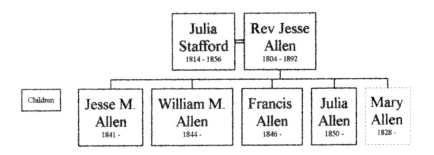

Mushcreek Cemetery

Harmony Fellowship Methodist Church Cemetery. Julia Stafford (Allen) Marker

Grave Marker McQueen Allen

Infant Daughter of Jesse & Julia Allen Harmony Fellowship Methodist Church Cemetery

Chapter Seven
MacQueen Allen

Reverend Jesse Allen's oldest son (and half-brother to my grandfather, Dr. A. Mayfield Allen) was named Jesse MacQueen Allen. He also became a preacher, ordained in 1878 at Abner Creek Baptist Church, Spartanburg County, South Carolina. McQueen Allen, the son of Julia Stafford and Jesse Allen, was born July 7, 1841 in Sumter, SC.

He joined the Baptist faith at Abner Creek Church after his father and family moved to the upstate of South Carolina. His mother died in 1856 and is buried in the cemetery of Harmony Fellowship Methodist Church, route 25, thirty miles south of Greenville, SC.

The ministry of Reverend McQueen Allen is discussed in Mann Batson's book, A History of the Upper Part of Greenville, South Carolina:

On Wednesday, April 29th, we went to Gowensville, Leaving home the afternoon before; we got as far on our journey as the home of Reverend McQueen Allen, seven miles above the city. Mr. Allen preaches to five churches, all located in Greenville County except Siloam, which is in Anderson. [Preachers' section, page 195.]

In the same article, McQueen and wife, Emma Neves Allen are presented a handmade quilt by one of the members of Mushcreek Church. The writer refers to the industriousness of the Reverend's wife, Emma:

"She looks well after her home. Since Christmas she has sold one hundred and thirty pounds of butter, produced from the milk of one cow; from which she has realized $26.00..."

The above quotes are from the newspaper, The Enterprise and Mountaineer, Issue of May 6th, 1891. McQueen Allen's age would have been fifty.

Page 562 of Batson's book describes the damage of a hailstorm which affected the people of the community of Mountain Creek Church. [Mr. John C. Allen] "lives on the farm of his father, Reverend Jesse M. Allen. And he has ten acres of splendid cotton that was literally riddled by the hailstones..." (Greenville Mountaineer, Issue of September 4, 1897.)

An earlier article (Enterprise and Mountaineer May 6, 1891) again speaking of John C. Allen, mentions he is a foster son of McQueen Allen. Family researcher, Postell Allen tells us 'Queen' Allen and his wife Emma adopted a son and a daughter. Quoting Postell: "Jesse McQueen Allen educated 30 orphan boys and girls."

My husband, Bill and I visited Mush Creek Cemetery and found the wrought-iron enclosed monuments of McQueen and Emma Allen. Mush Creek Church Cemetery is small and is located off the main highway and the bustling traffic! It is in a peaceful, serene setting on a little incline across the road from a creek. The memory of its country setting is even more appealing because of the natural scenic qualities found there. Pictures were taken by Bill of the grave markers—-pictures for my 'Allen' genealogical documentation and for appreciation of this historical site!

Descendants of John Gates

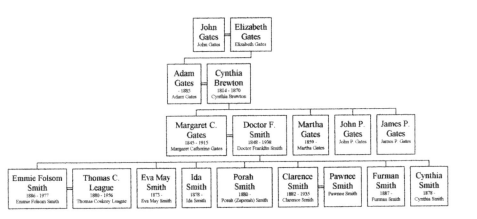

Chapter Eight
Gates and Brewton

Five years after the birth of my paternal great grandfather Jesse Allen, my maternal great- great grandfather, Adam Gates was born. The year was 1809 and the place was Orangeburg, South Carolina. The contrast between these two men is striking! Jesse Allen was supposedly "Irish" and Adam Gates was definitely "German." My grandmother, Emmie Smith League, described him as a "full blooded Dutchman who couldn't speak plain English!"

Edna Westmoreland, Woodruff genealogist, in letter dated August 26, 1993, made these comments: "I do not have parents [of Adam Gates] but they were German and were in Orangeburg County before coming to this area, along with the Switzers and Brandenburgs."

From records of Saint Matthews Lutheran Church, Calhoun County, South Carolina are many Gates' families and among these is Adam Gates and his parents, John and Elizabeth Gates. It is in this church that Adam Gates' baptism took place—October 28, 1809.

Internet information posted November 19, 1999 on the "Gates Family Forum" speaks of a Bible at St. Matthews Lutheran Church, Cameron, SC, wherein: "The following was written on a fly leaf in the Bible: 'John Anthony Menicken b. May 1785 at Cologne on the River Rhein…was married to Elizabeth Gates 2 Mar. 1809." The source, according to Robert Cady Gates, (writer of two volumes of Gates' Families in America) is "Old Southern Bible Records" (1974) by Memory Aldrich Lester. Mr. Gates, speaking to another Gates' researcher, Mike Morgan, says:
"I believe you have information showing that this Elizabeth Gates was a daughter of Martin and Mary Gates."

The message posted November 18, 1999 by Mike Morgan lists the descendants of George Gates (1723-1804) who resided in

Orangeburg, SC. His son, Martin Gates (1754-1806) had a daughter, Elizabeth Gates. All were connected to St. Matthews Lutheran Church. The next statement is important to me: "The descendants of George Gates: Martin Gates (1754-1806) married Mary; their daughter Elizabeth married John Anthony Menicken."

Please note Adam Gates' mother was Elizabeth Gates, daughter of Martin and Mary Gates. She married John Anthony Menicken; yet Adam Gates is christened as 'son of John and Mary Gates.' There is the question, should Adam Gates be Adam Menicken?

If someone reading this can verify that Adam's father is indeed, John Gates, please do so. I'm very happy with my Gates' ancestors. but what became of John Menicken? Maybe it was just easier to use the Gates' name rather than to explain an erroneous entry.

In the Switzer/Woodruff area of SC were Brewton and Skinner families. Cynthia Brewton married Adam Gates. She was born in 1814 and died 1870. Her parents were Agness and Philip Brewton. Philip was the grandson of Samuel Bruton, the 'Regulator' born 1700 Virginia and died after 1763 in Anson, NC.

Genealogist, Marie Olson, of Charleston, SC was kind enough to mail an ancestral chart of the Bruton family (letter dated July 10, 1999.) Her ancestor, Jacob Brewton, is also a grandson of Samuel Bruton, as well as a cousin to Philip Bruton. In a letter from Marie Keenan Olson dated 19 July 1999 she stated: " It is believed that Samuel Bruton, the 'Regulator' was the father of David Bruton (born about 1740 in Virginia and Married about 1761 in Anson, North Carolina) who died in Spartanburg, South Carolina 15 December 1815.

David Brewton's son, Phillip Brewton (born13 Sept. 1778; died 17 June 1861—Woodruff, SC) was the father of Cynthia

Brewton who married Adam Gates. Cynthia and Adam were the grandparents of my grandmother, Emmie Smith League.

Back to Cynthia Brewton and Adam Gates; two daughters were born to them: Martha Elizabeth (1839-1930) and Margaret Catherine (1845-1915,) Martha Elizabeth married James Calvin Skinner (1833-1908) and Margaret Catherine (Maggie) married D. F. Smith (1848-1938.)

The Skinner-Gates Family History has copies of the following: Adam Gates' Will (1872); the obituary for Cynthia Brewton Gates (1870); Gates-Brewton ancestral chart; the obituary for Martha Gates Skinner (1930); Tombstone inscriptions for Philip and Agness Brewton; the Will of David Bruton, Senior; and much more concerning the family of James Calvin and Martha Elizabeth (Aunt Matt) Skinner. (8, 18-20).

In the beginning of the Skinner-Gates History, is a picture of Aunt Matt Skinner and her husband James Calvin Skinner. This picture reminded me of a family photo portrait of Maggie Gates and D. F. Smith. My grandmother Emmie Smith and all her siblings are in this portrait—as well as Granny's Aunt Lucy who is on the porch in a chair. Aunt Lucy (Brewton or Gates, I'm not sure) was an invalid who had been crippled all her life. Granny spoke of Aunt Lucy and her strong faith. As Aunt Lucy was dying, Granny said her Aunt smiled and told her she saw Jesus!

Notable is the resemblance in the pictures between Aunt Matt Skinner and her sister, Maggie Smith, my great grandmother. My grandmother, Emmie was just a girl of eleven or twelve, when the photo was made. She was dressed in a white dress and had long, light-brown curls. This must have been before Emmie had 'scarlet fever' and lost most of her hair. Another picture at age seventeen portrays a beautiful young woman who has lovely dark hair.

The Smith family portrait was made in front of the old Smith home place, later the Franklin Smith home on Anderson-

Ridge Road near Batesville. The mother, Maggie not a large woman; her hair back in a bun and 'a fine figure' for a woman who had born seven children—stood by her seated husband, D.F. Smith with her hand on his shoulder. There were two sons, Clarence and Furman. The sisters were Ida, Cynthia, Porah and Eva.

My mother was named for her grandmother—Margaret or Annie Margaret. Sometimes my grandmother, Emmie called my mother, Margaret or Maggie—usually with affection and perhaps at other times, exasperation— she'd say, "Oh, Maggie."

These women: my mother, grandmother and great grand-mother were unconventional women. This is an understatement! My great grandmother [Maggie] smoked a small corncob pipe. My mother, Anne League Allen fit the description of the 'flapper girl' in the 20's, when she did the "Charleston" on the stage of the Carolina Theater in Greenville, SC and won a prize! How fun loving my mother and grandmother were and all of my mother's family.

I can truthfully say, without a doubt, my Granny, has been one of the strongest influences in my life. An unforgettable character, outspoken and quick tempered; there were many dimensions to her. A person with plenty of 'back-bone', she knew what 'work' was! Milking cows, doing chores, cooking, raising seven children, and reading her Bible every day, caring for her family and her neighbors;—she enjoyed reading, movies, cigarettes and Pepsi's! I can see her down on her knees scrubbing the kitchen floor and whistling or singing hymns all the while! The picture of Granny kneeling by the bedside, saying her prayers every morning and evening is more than a memory—I think of it as a legacy!

Ancestors of Anne League

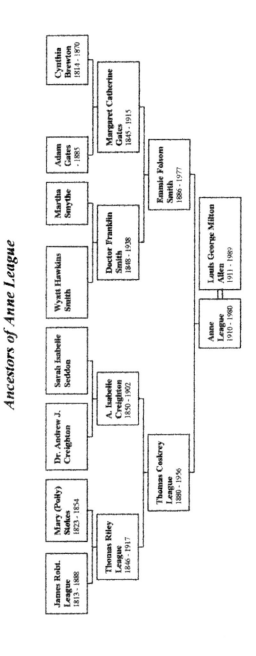

Emmie Smith

The Nine Chimney House
(1840's to 1977)

This house was built by Joseph Stairley, an English immigrant.
It was the main house on his 2,000 acre plantation on Old
Scuffletown Road. All of this building was put together with
wooden pegs and square nails, all hand made on the site.
One of the most unusual features of the house is that it is
weatherboarded with planks 10 to 12 inches wide, running
straight up and down. Where they are joined together, the
cracks are covered with round circle split strip, now called
half-round molding. The house has four gables, one on each
side. Three of the gables have three small chimneys each,
thus the name "The Nine Chimney House".

From the History compiled by:
Mays League Greene (Mrs. Leonard)
And Preserved by Mrs. Annie C. Stenhouse

Dr. Thomas Riley League 'Belle' League siblings of Thomas Costrly League

Dr. Thomas Riley League

Isabelle Creighton League

A. Creighton League

Thomas C. League
(Papa, as a young man)

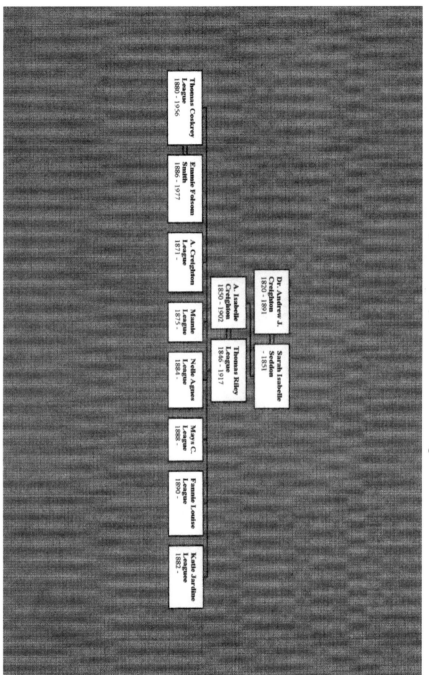

Hourglass Tree of Dr. Andrew J. Creighton

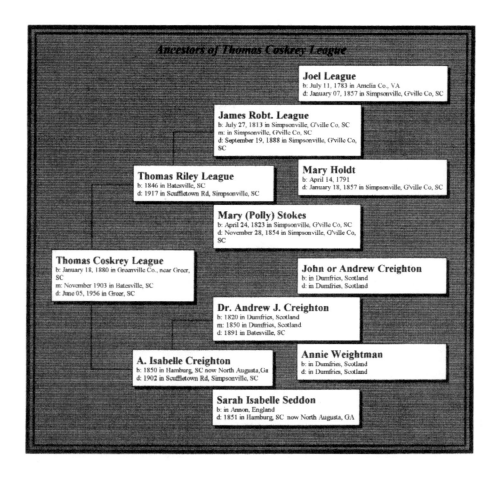

Ancestors of Thomas Coskrey League

Joel League
b: July 11, 1783 in Amelia Co., VA
d: January 07, 1857 in Simpsonville, G'ville Co, SC

James Robt. League
b: July 27, 1813 in Simpsonville, G'ville Co, SC
m: in Simpsonville, G'ville Co, SC
d: September 19, 1888 in Simpsonville, G'ville Co, SC

Thomas Riley League
b: 1846 in Batesville, SC
d: 1917 in Scuffletown Rd, Simpsonville, SC

Mary Holdt
b: April 14, 1791
d: January 18, 1857 in Simpsonville, G'ville Co, SC

Mary (Polly) Stokes
b: April 24, 1823 in Simpsonville, G'ville Co, SC
d: November 28, 1854 in Simpsonville, G'ville Co, SC

Thomas Coskrey League
b: January 18, 1880 in Greenville Co., near Greer, SC
m: November 1903 in Batesville, SC
d: June 05, 1956 in Greer, SC

John or Andrew Creighton
b: in Dumfries, Scotland
d: in Dumfries, Scotland

Dr. Andrew J. Creighton
b: 1820 in Dumfries, Scotland
m: 1850 in Dumfries, Scotland
d: 1891 in Batesville, SC

A. Isabelle Creighton
b: 1850 in Hamburg, SC now North Augusta, Ga
d: 1902 in Scuffletown Rd, Simpsonville, SC

Annie Weightman
b: in Dumfries, Scotland
d: in Dumfries, Scotland

Sarah Isabelle Seddon
b: in Annon, England
d: 1851 in Hamburg, SC now North Augusta, GA

Chapter Nine
The Scotsman,
Dr. Andrew John Creighton
and the Leagues

As already mentioned, my maternal GATES-SMITH line includes my German great great grandfather, Adam Gates (b.1809). His people came from the Rhine river valley of Germany. From my paternal ALLEN-MAYFIELD line is the 'Irishman', great grandfather, Jesse Allen (b.1804) whose people came to the United States by way of Ireland. Now, a Scotsman merits our attention—the maternal grandfather of Papa League, Dr. Andrew John Creighton!

Dr. Andrew J. Creighton was born December 12, 1820 in Dumfries, Scotland. "When Andrew John Creighton was nineteen (1839), he and two Oxford University class mates made the decision to come to America." (Greene, Mays League, Unpublished League History, 1980). With classmates, Mr. Newell and Mr. Coskrey, Andrew Creighton began his journey on a cattle boat from Liverpool. Landing at Jacksonville, Florida, the three men continued on to Savannah, Georgia and then to Augusta, Georgia. That August, Andrew Creighton "entered medical school to finish his previous study of medicine." (Green, 1980). This information was written in a family account by my great aunt, Mays League Greene, sister of my grandfather, Thomas Coskrey League and the granddaughter of Dr. Andrew J. Creighton.

The LEAGUE-CREIGHTON ancestral branches were passed to me from my mother, Anne League Allen through her father, Thomas Coskrey League—notice the middle name of her father—Coskrey! Evidently there was a strong connection from classmate, Mr. Coskrey and the family of Andrew Creighton and his daughter, Annie Isabelle Creighton League.

After ten years in America, Dr. Creighton went back to Scotland and there married his sweetheart, Sarah Isabelle Seddon (1848). As a wedding present, Dr. Creighton presented his wife with an instrument, known as the "Glass Harmonica." It passed from generation to generation until my Aunt Sally, Sarah Isabelle League Connelly received it. Now it belongs to my cousin, Steven Connelly.

Dr. Andrew J. Creighton and Sarah Isabelle Seddon had one child, Annie Isabelle Creighton. She was born August 24, 1850 in North Augusta [called Hamburg at the time] Georgia. Annie was almost a year old when her mother died. Sarah Seddon Creighton was buried in Magnolia Cemetery in North Augusta. Annie gained a stepmother when her father married Mary Montgomery. A half-sister, Mary Montgomery Creighton was born from Dr. Creighton's second marriage.

Later, the family moved to upstate South Carolina "six miles below Greer, SC; five miles from Cashville, in Spartanburg County." (Greene, 1980). Dr. Creighton practiced medicine and ran a country store. He raised sheep, utilizing the thread mill at Batesville as a "ready market for his wool." (Greene, 1980).

After his daughters married and his second wife died, Dr. Creighton lived with daughter, Annie Creighton League and her husband, Dr. Thomas Riley League. At the time, he was appointed U.S. Postmaster of Greer, SC and "served in this position some four or five years before retiring because of his age." (Greene, 1980).

The Creightons were of the Presbyterian faith—as were many Scots who left Scotland—and upon his death (December 1890) he was buried beside his second wife in the Antioch Presbyterian Church Cemetery (Spartanburg County, SC, near Cashville)

Although nothing is known of his early life, Andrew J. Creighton sounds like a remarkable man—someone with an adventurous spirit and an industrious nature!! According to Aunt Mays Greene: "after finishing medical school in Augusta, Ga., he located in Graniteville and set up practice for the town and country. He also worked in the town bank!" (Ibid.) A shrewd Scotsman, ever mindful of expanding himself, he saw opportunities in the upstate and willingly left North Augusta to put down 'roots' in Batesville, S.C.

The wedding of Dr. Creighton's daughter, Annie Creighton and Dr. Thomas Riley League took place at Ebenezer Church at Batesville—(as did the marriage of my grandfather and grandmother, Tom and Emmie Smith League.) Another dimension developed in our ancestry with this marriage—the purely Scot Creightons joined with the French Huguenot Leagues. The Leagues, originally from France, were supposedly from the Bordeaux region of France. Before coming to Virginia, there was a possible intermingling with Scots/German and English. The League history dates back to Amelia County, Va. in the 1700's. Ancestor James League (1725-1814) and his wife, Mary Anne Marshbanks (1735-1817) are recorded in the family Bible of James Robert League, Sr. The Bible is owned by the Britt League family of Richmond, Va. It was published in 1806, in Amelia County, Virginia.

Joel League (11 July 1783; 7 Jan 1857) and Mary Anne Holdt (14 Apr 1791; 18 Jan 1857) came to South Carolina from Virginia with William Stokes and his wife, Nancy Phillips. William and Nancy Phillips Stokes were the parents of 'Polly' Stokes who married James Robert League—later known as Robert League. Robert League was the father of Dr. Thomas Riley League and the son of Joel and Mary Holdt League.

The background of the Stokes' and Phillips' is unknown but may have been Scot-Irish or English. By the time we get to our generation, the French blood has diluted, considerably. How nice if the politeness and reserve, characteristic of Papa League's family, remained with our generation and those to come!

Papa's sister, Aunt Mays Greene, relates how her father, Thomas Riley League volunteered as a sixteen year old to fight in the Civil War. After about two years, he was wounded by a burst cannon ball. The injury was in his right side, near his waist. He was treated and hospitalized in the hospital (Augusta, Ga.) where he remained for approximately six months. Upon his release, he decided to study medicine—but before entering medical school, he studied with Dr. William 'Billy' Austin. (Ibid.)

Aunt Mays words: "Father went to Medical School, close to the end of the war, and entered as a second year student. He had a brilliant mind, was active and very observing; was small in stature, about five feet four inches tall and weighed around 120-125 pounds."

Dr. League set up his medical practice in the Batesville-Pelham area of South Carolina. While living at Batesville, the first four children of Dr. Tom and 'Belle' League were born—the oldest named Andrew Creighton League. On moving to another home (now known as the Victor Smith place), the family increased by five more: Papa (Thomas C. League) and his four sisters. The next move was to Greer, S.C. and two more sisters (Mays League and Louise League) were added to the family. Aunt Mays wrote the League History. Cousin DeWitt Stenhouse' wife, Annie typed and copied all the material for the League History. DeWitt's mother was Aunt Louise. Aunt Mays was the mother of Theresa Greene Bramlette, and Tommy Greene. Aunt Mays died sometime between 1980 and 1985. Her son Tommy Greene died after 1989 but I don't have the exact years for their deaths. More detailed information on the siblings of my grandfather, Thomas Coskrey League can be found in the League History of Mays League Greene.

Over in Simpsonville, SC, Dr. Thos Riley League's brother, Uncle Pliney League was also a doctor. (Hipps, Frank. Memories of Simpsonville, 1996: ii, 34-35). This area was where Dr. Thos Riley League was born and where his father, Robert League lived.

Not far from Simpsonville, on Scuffletown Road, was the 'old Stairley Place' which Dr. Tom decided to buy. He may have wanted to get back to his 'League roots' (his father having died September 1888) or he may have found the home appealing because of its 'Nine Chimneys' and 600 acres! Whatever his desire, the move was made from Greer when Papa (Thos C. League) was eight years old and Aunt Louise was one month old. The medical practice for Dr. League now covered "both upper and lower Greenville County." (Greene, League History, 1980).

In 1900, Dr. League retired and in 1902, his wife, 'Belle' died. In 1906, one 'last' move brought Dr. Tom to Greenville, S.C. During the years 1888-1890, he served as a member of the S.C. House of Representatives from Greenville County and in the years 1909-1910, he was elected again. (Batson, Mann. A History of Upper Greenville County).

My grandmother, Emmie Smith League, respected her father-in-law, Dr. Tom. She always spoke well of him. Once, speaking of the Leagues, Granny told how Dr. League would take out a handkerchief and dust off a chair before sitting down. Was this a part of his upbringing or was he just a fastidious person? Maybe he had the trait I always had. I never wanted to get my hands dirty!! Children usually enjoy getting muddy and playing in the dirt but I never really enjoyed getting dirty! But getting back to the Leagues, Granny and Papa lived with Dr. Tom and Belle League when they first married. Before their marriage, Emmie's family farmed on Dr. League's land. Seeing young Tom League (Thomas C.) riding his horse over the fields so impressed Emmie Smith that I'm sure she 'set her cap for him.' She probably thought these words (used many times over the years): "Oh, that gentleman-born, Tom League!"

Chapter Ten
Gretna Green- Dumfries, Scotland

Let's turn to the southwestern corner of Scotland, an area "that has always stayed apart from the Scottish mainstream…" This area encompasses Dumfries, Galloway and Ayrshire. (Bentley, James and Anne Midgette, <u>Nelles Guide, 1997</u>. p. 87.)

"Further east, on the English border, the **Old Toll House** in Gretna is the first house in Scotland for anyone coming up from the south." English couples, after the 16th century were able to forego a church wedding and be married in Scotland in Gretna Green's Old Blacksmith Shop, a frequent wedding site. All that was needed was just a declaration of the couple's wish to be married. "…marriage by declaration became illegal in 1856" (Ibid.)

My husband, Bill and I were able to go to Gretna Green while on a trip to London and Scotland in 1994. A picture was made of our tour group in the Blacksmith Shop. Another was made of Bill and me under the 'kissing gate.' Yes, we were kissing!

Later I realized we were in the Dumfries area. I've wondered if this might be the place where Dr. Andrew Creighton and Sarah Isabelle Seddon were married. Her place of birth, Annan— England or Scotland. Could it be Annan, Scotland? This is the area of Dumfries where ancestor Dr. Andrew Creighton was born! Their marriage took place in 1848.

Note: Information on the "Dumfries and Galloway History of Annan, Scotland" can be found on the web site, http://www.annan.org.uk/history/printable and html.

Ancestors of Louis George Milton Allen

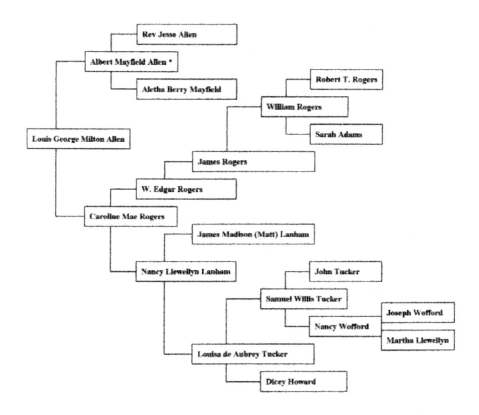

Chapter Eleven
Lanham – Rogers - Allen

Nancy Llewellyn Lanham (1851-1897) was another grand-parent my Father never knew. Her grave marker is in the Walnut Grove Cemetery, Roebuck, S.C. The marker for her husband, Wm. Edgar Rogers (1845-1913) is in the same Cemetery. Nancy was the first wife of Edgar Rogers and the mother of Mae Rogers, my father's mother. Caroline Mae Rogers was born in 1875 and died in 1921, when my father, Louis Allen was only ten. She was 46 years old and had four children from her marriage to Dr. Albert Mayfield Allen. The siblings of Louis G. Allen: Albert Lanham Allen (1907 -1978), Marion Columbus Allen (1914 - 1995), and Annie Josephine Allen (1909 - 1988).   Mae Rogers' first marriage was to Wade Layton, who died 1904; a son named Hugh was born, possibly 1902. Dr. Allen would not allow this son to come into his home after his marriage to Mae Rogers Layton. Hugh Layton was raised by relatives of Mae (May) Rogers Layton Allen.

In 1906, Dr. A. M. Allen's first wife Emily Josephine died. She was the sister of Caroline Mae Rogers. From this marriage were three children: Ellyn Allen (1900 –before 1978), Harold Allen (1903 -1921) and Jessica Allen (1905 - 1993).

When the second marriage took place, first cousins became half-brothers and half-sisters. My father's half-sister and first cousin, Ellyn became especially close because she was the oldest and helped care for the younger children. Ellyn's name came from her grandmother, Nancy Llewellyn Lanham (Rogers).

Ellyn Allen became a teacher, as was her stepmother, Mae Rogers Allen. She married a Methodist Minister, Reverend Wallace Gleaton. This fine and distinguished man brought balance, harmony and happiness to all. Considering the harshness of Dr. A. M. Allen, to his children, it is understandable that his children would seek a peaceful environment in their respective homes.

Having visited my cousin, Carolyn Gleaton, Uncle Wallace and Aunt Ellyn; their home presented an ideal family!   At the time, Uncle Wallace was pastor of the Methodist Church in Sumter, SC. The Church, parsonage and town made quite an impression on this little girl, whose home was out in the 'country' from Greer, SC and who attended a 'country church,' and a 'country school.' I was envious! You could walk from the parsonage to the public library and even check out books!!! Carolyn and I were the same age, born in the same month and we were both, 'only' children (no brothers or sisters). It interesting to note that Carolyn named her daughter after her mother's aunt, (Mae) and her mother, Ellyn—Mae Ellyn!

Often my Dad and his brothers would reminisce about their childhood and their father's lack of affection. I think of the sweet, sensitive nature of my father and I'm sure he wondered why his father denied simple pleasures to his family! Work and chores, schoolwork and learning—those were the priorities! If we had the knowledge of the early life of Albert Mayfield Allen, it might be easier to understand him. We know that the household of Rev. Jesse Allen was 'needy' in material things. From a statement by Uncle Marion, quoting Dr. Allen, his father: "How could Jesse go to sleep at night knowing his children were hungry?" Having been deprived of any kind of luxury in life and having to walk long distances for education— somehow managing to go to medical school in Augusta, Georgia— Dr. Albert Mayfield Allen knew what it meant to be disciplined and what it meant to sacrifice! Still his children looked back with painful memories of their father. My Dad referred to him as " The Old Gent."   He was born in 1867 and was forty-four years old when my father, Louis Allen was born. Dr. Allen's father, Rev. Jesse Allen was Sixty-three when Albert Mayfield Allen was born. Albert Mayfield Allen's siblings were Henry Milton Allen, Columbus Allen and Manora Jane Allen. Half-brother, Rev. J MacQueen Allen has been mentioned previously; others were Frank Allen, William McKenzie Allen, and Julia Allen (Waters). Their mother was Julia Stafford Allen, who died in 1856. Another half-sister was Mary Allen, but Julia Stafford Allen was not her mother! Rev. Jesse was married before his marriage to Julia Stafford. This marriage was in Fayette County, Georgia, before Jesse came to Sumter, S.C.

(1830-1840 Censuses, Fayette County, GA). Mary Allen was born 1828. She married Will Rhodes of Spartanburg County, SC, November 6, 1861. (Marriage Notice, Brent Holcombe).

Brothers of Dr. Allen who fought in the Civil War were Privates: Francis Allen, McQueen J. Allen, and Wm. Allen. They were all in the 2nd Regiment of S.C.V., Calvary, Company E, (Landrum, History of Spartanburg County, (1900) page 716).

Lack of proper nutrition can result in health problems, one of which is "Pellagra." A lack of certain vitamins, especially vitamin C can cause mental deficiencies. Did this play a role in the mental illness of my aunt, Annie Josephine Allen, Daddy's sister? She was diagnosed as 'Schizophrenic,' and was institutionalized—first in Columbia, SC and later, in Greenville, SC. She was the librarian in the State Mental Hospital (Columbia, SC) when I first saw her. This was after I married and had children. We conversed normally and had a nice visit. Later, we would see her from time to time but my Dad visited her regularly at Grady Hipp Retirement Home (Greenville, SC), where she often played piano for Hymn-Singing.

She was a student at Converse College studying piano when her 'breakdown' occurred. She remained at home for some years and stayed with half-sister, Ellyn on occasion but Dr. Allen realized she needed medical supervision and a provision was made for her in his will. At her death (May 16, 1988), a graveside service was conducted by Uncle Marion Allen who referred to Josephine as "one of God's Angels."

Dr. Albert Lanham Allen, my Dad's brother was a radiologist. He married Julia Winn and lived many years in Winchester, Kentucky Before America entered World War II, Uncle Albert served as a doctor with the British Army; he later transferred to the American Army. He lived in Japan and India for a time. Possessing a photographic memory, he often quoted passages from literature. Always colorful and charming, his presence commanded attention! When he died, Aunt Julia said, "I've lost my Encyclopedia."

A memoir written by Albert Allen, <u>Blue Days and Fair</u>, describes the countryside Five miles out from Spartanburg, SC, where the "Union and Columbia branch of the Southern Railway" was located. "The rural farm house" where the Allen family lived was approximately "a half mile further away." Speaking of himself, Uncle Albert says, "Thanks to my mother, a former teacher, I was reading at five years." "...yet I could recite from the age of four the best stanzas of a hymn, ...heard not more than twice perhaps—and at six I had memorized some of the best poems in the English Tongue." Continuing, "the little white school house stood on a lot donated by our Sire [Dr. A. M. Allen]; the school itself was in sight of our own wooden frame house. The lot had been a small parcel of our forty acres on the 'old Thomson Place' of Revolutionary War fame." "...known as the Thomson School, it was 'the sole center of learning between Cedar Spring and the ruins of the Wofford Iron Works...'" Teachers came by way of a streetcar from Spartanburg, getting off the tram, they walked about two miles to reach the school. ..."the years slowly passed. The little white schoolhouse was gradually losing ground. "The Consolidated School—had taken away some of the younger classes, and I was among the first to go." The new school was at Foster's Tavern. After an eight-month session, I was ready to join my brother, (the next year) in walking to the streetcar. "I began my first experience in the nearby City Schools." [Harold] was in his last year of High School and young Albert was entering the fifth grade.

Albert Allen's brother, Marion C. Allen, edited this memoir: "Albert for some :reason has changed the name of our oldest brother, Harold, to Hanley.." J. Harold Allen was born July 4, 1902 and was lost at sea in the spring of 1921—"a sailor in the U. S. Navy Following World War I."

Chapter Twelve
Marion C. Allen

From a sermon in the First Congregational Church of Topeka, Kansas, July 23, 1978, Rev. M. C. Allen speaks on "Detour Ahead!" He asks: "Do you remember the old commencement addresses at graduation time?" In the next paragraph, Uncle Marion reveals a personal 'detour,' a time when financial problems could end his pursuit of a college degree. His words: "In 1932, the year I graduated from high school, our class heard such an address. What followed? I managed to struggle through the freshman year at college until the money ran out. That meant a red light and an arrow pointed to the side. A new and hard experience it was for our family. It was a grateful young man who got the chance to make 30 dollars a month in the C.C.C. (Civilian Conservation Corps) the next fall. One day as we were shoveling the red soil into a truck for the building of a road, I spoke of that commencement address to a fellow worker, 'And he didn't say a thing about the C.C.C., did he?' was his reply."

Later, Marion returns to this experience: "The experience of being an unwilling college dropout left me bitter, for all of my brothers and sisters had been able to go through college without interruption. Yet in the C.C.C. Camp, I learned a great deal from people who had little education yet who knew how to share generously from their meager stores. Then there was Chaplain C. R. Watkins, whose assistant I became. We used to study Greek together, and he became a spiritual father in my hour of need."

Senior Oratorical Contest

In 1937, Marion C. Allen "was awarded the Durham Medal after the decision of the judges was rendered," (newspaper article, "M.C. Allen of Sumter wins Furman Oratorical Contest," Greenville News-Piedmont, Greenville, SC)

Later he graduated with honors from the Yale School of Divinity in New Haven, Connecticut and was ordained (1940) at the First Baptist Church in Waterbury, Conn., in the American Church Denomination. On July 31, 1943, he married Eleanor Burt, a graduate of Oberlin Conservatory of Music and "a teacher of public school music." (Obituary, Rev. Marion (Sam) Allen).

A move in 1947 brought Marion and Eleanor to Beaufort, South Carolina, where he served as pastor of Beaufort Baptist Church. Three years later the Allens were in Clemson, SC and Marion was pastor of Clemson Baptist Church. After six years, the family unit included four children who along with Marion and Eleanor re-located to Lawrence, Kansas! That must have been quite a turn-around!! There were two girls and two boys—Marian, the oldest; Burt and Bob, next, and baby Louise, last. The year was 1956 and the new church was the First Baptist Church. Marion served this church as Senior Pastor until 1976.

In a newspaper article, "Pastor to deliver farewell sermon," Tonda Rush (J-W Staff Writer) quoted Rev. M. C. Allen: "Most people don't realize a minister's call isn't like something out of the blue, like a clap of thunder. For most of us who take it seriously, it is arrived at after much serious consideration. I considered teaching; in fact I went to Yale to teach..."But it was as if the Lord said to me, 'you'll read your books—anyway. I'm going to put you out where the people are.'"

Earning a Master's in English at Kansas University, Marion taught English courses at various times at the University of Kansas and, not surprisingly wrote a book, <u>AVoice Not Our Own.</u>

Uncle Marion traveled to South Carolina to officiate at the funerals of my mother, Anne League Allen; Marion's sister (and my aunt) Josephine Allen; and my father, Louis G. Allen. The years were respectively, 1980, 1988 and 1989. He also conducted a memorial service for his sister, Jessica Allen in 1993. She had lived in Washington, D.C. and worked for the government in the printing department. The service for Jessica was held at Walnut Grove, Roebuck, South Carolina.

Uncle Marion wrote to my father, Louis on June 10, 1988, after the funeral of Aunt Josephine conducted at Hillcrest Memorial Gardens, Greer, S.C.

"I was glad that no stranger who would have had neither understanding nor affection was in charge of the service. I was also glad that you could get Carolyn [Cox] to sing. In its own way, with the little group gathered at the graveside, it was rather memorable. I'll always be grateful for what you did through the years for Josephine.

"We Allens are remarkably poor at expressing our affection but I'm sure it's there all the same. Certainly, I owe much to you and your care since I was but a tot. You were always kind and under-standing as an older brother should be when the difference is three years, three months, and thirteen days. Now we are both toddlers again but with a lot of pains that keep it from being as much fun."

Note: In just ten months, my father, Louis Allen changed his earth-ly residence for an eternal residence—April 8, 1989.

**Walnut Grove, A Memorial Service for Jessica Allen
At left standing Henry Cox (son of Carolyn), Uncle Marion
and Aunt Eleanor, friend Mr. Purcer, kneeling in front
Carolyn Cox, Toya Harvey.**

Chapter Thirteen
Prayer by Rev. Marion C. Allen

Graveside Service
for Dr. Albert Lanham Allen
August 13, 1978
Florence, Alabama

Almighty God, from whom we come, unto whom we return, and in whom, while we tarry here on earth, we live and move and have our being; we praise thee for thy joys; its friendships and fellowships. We thank thee for the ties that bind us to one another and to thee, and for thy guiding hand along the way of our pilgrimage.

We give thee thanks especially for this thy child, Dr. Albert Lanham Allen, recalling all in him that made others love him. We bless thee for all good and gracious influences in home and training, for all that ministered to his best life. Especially we remember with gratitude his mother and his father, the kindness and care of an older sister, and for others who instilled in him from the time of infancy, a love of the good, the true, and the beautiful. We are thankful for the positive influences in college and beyond, especially for his dear wife Julia.

For all helpfulness that has passed from his life into the lives of others, we thank thee; for his ministry as a physician, for his keen mind and his lively sense of humor, his delight in music and poetry, and in all things bright and beautiful. We who have received so much from him bow before thee with warm appreciation and thankfulness.

We thank thee too that deep in the human heart is an unquenchable trust that life does not end with death; that the Father, who made us, will not leave us in the dust, but will care for us beyond the bounds of vision, even as he has cared for us in our earthly life. We praise thy name that this our hope has been so wondrously confirmed in the life and words and resurrection of our Lord Jesus Christ.

Grant us we beseech thee, the comfort now of thine assured presence and the quiet ministries of thy Holy Spirit. The more we perceive that the things which are seen as temporal, so much the surer make us that the things which are not seen are eternal. Teach us to live as those who are prepared to die; and then thy summons comes, soon or late, teach us to die as those who are prepared to live; that living or dying we may be with thee, and that nothing henceforward, either in life or in death, shall be able to separate us from thy love which is in Christ Jesus our Lord.

Rev. Marion C. Allen

Albert Allen

Rev. Jesse Allen

Doctor Albert Mayfield Allen M.D.
Reverend Henry Milton Allen
Columbus Allen
Manora Jane Allen

Aletha Berry Mayfield

Chapter Fourteen
Dr. Albert Mayfield Allen

Known to many as 'Mayfield' Allen or Dr. A. M. Allen-Mayfield was his mother's maiden name. Little information, if any, is available about his childhood. We can only surmise that as the son of Reverend Jesse Allen Mayfield, he and his siblings faced many hardships. The family lived on land that was declared, "tax free." It was not farmable land. A rock quarry covered part of the land. This meant the preacher and his family had to rely on the generous help of neighbors and church members to provide for them from time to time. Evidently, Mayfield was not afraid of hard work and knew the meaning of sacrifice; how else could he accomplish what he did with his life? In the years he was studying medicine, how did he manage to get to a medical college? Where did he find the finances for his education?

The 1900 census for Spartanburg, SC, listed Dr. Albert Mayfield Allen as head of household; his wife is Josephine and baby daughter, Ellyn. Brother-in-law, Will Rogers is listed in the home and together they operate a dairy. Mayfield is 33 years old and Josephine is 23 years old; baby Ellyn is 6 months old.

From a poor background, but with a dominant, spirited father, Mayfield may have inherited traits of perseverance and thriftiness. Ambitious, and striving toward a life goal of financial security, he knew the necessity and value of an education. His emphasis on 'learning' and its importance was conveyed to Mayfield Allen's family.

Serving as a country doctor and doctor/pharmacist in the mills of Clifton and Glendale, he left Abner Creek Baptist Church and joined Glendale Baptist Church 1893, the year after his father, Rev. Jesse Allen died. Mayfield was 26 years old.

A History of Abner's Creek Church" 1832-1904, speaks of revival services at Abner Creek Baptist Church (August 1878) and The meetings "resulted in the addition of forty-seven members by experience and baptism." [This information came from Program Notes from ceremony on 16th of Sept. 1979.]   Reverend Jesse was 74 years old at the time and his son, A. Mayfield Allen was eleven years old!

A. Mayfield Allen and his sister, Manora Jane were the youngest children from the marriage of Aletha Berry Mayfield and Jesse Allen. Two other brothers were Columbus Allen and Henry Milton Allen. Columbus died after the Civil War. He contracted blood poison while doing construction work at the capitol in Columbia, SC.

Henry Milton Allen, ordained at Abner Creek Baptist Church as a minister (1878) served a number of churches around Anderson and one of these was Starr Baptist Church. Eventually he went to Texas and had a rather large ministry there. More about Henry Milton is found in the research of Postell Allen, his grandson. I'm grateful for the use of the material loaned to me by Pansy Allen, wife of Postell Allen, Jr. {Pansy is the sister of friends, Ramona Lewis and Cindy Hunter, Easley Baptist Church.}

Mayfield's regard for his brother, Henry Milton is shown in naming my father, Louis George Milton Allen. Dr. Allen named his first child, Jessica for himself. For reasons unknown, none of the daughters of A. Mayfield Allen were named for his mother, Aletha or his sister, Manora Jane.

Postell Allen's research with neighbors of Jesse Allen (Mr.McHugh and   Mr.McClimon) states: "A. Mayfield Allen became a doctor, graduating from the University of GA and the University of Ohio." I have not been able to find records, personally; it is known he served as a doctor in Glendale (Glendale, A Pictorial History. P.65). Referring again to notes of Postell Allen,

"He settled to practice medicine at Clifton #1, Clifton #2 and Clifton #3 near Spartanburg, SC. He also ran a dairy and a drug store."

It is interesting that "In 1880, [Dexter E.] Converse had formed the Clifton Manufacturing Company, a very successful enterprise that ultimately would develop three large textile manufacturing plants on the Pacolet River a few miles from Glendale."(Glendale, p.17). From the same source we find: "Few records exist about community life in the early years of Glendale. Among the earliest visitors to the region was Methodist Bishop Francis Asbury, who traveled through the upstate annually between 1787 and 1814. His diary includes these notations: 'On March 26, 1795, 'crossed Pacolet River. My body is weak, and so is my faith for this part of the vineyard.... This country improves in cultivation, wickedness, mills and stills'..." (p.12)

"Around 1900, an electric streetcar system began operation from Spartanburg through Glendale and on to Clifton Mill #1 and Converse. The cars transported both passengers and freight. Railway sidings were used to load and unload freight at Glendale and also on Clifton-Glendale Road. The Spartanburg Railway, Gas and Electric Company built the system. The line from Spartanburg to Glendale ran along Pine Street to Country Club Road." (Glendale p.21). Service was discontinued in 1935: "The last streetcar ran from Spartanburg to Glendale, April 16, 1935, when the system was replaced by buses." (p.21)

Mr. Paul Crocker, historian for the Glendale Community and one of the authors of Glendale, a Pictorial History, (correspondence dated May 5, 1993) presented the following information from the Glendale Baptist Church Record Book:
March 4, 1894
Dr. A. M. Allen in consultation with his own pastor finally and kindly declined to accept ordination (Deacon) stating that he feared that his business as a physician would prevent

his discharging the duties devolving upon a deacon of the church as should be done. Then the pastor in behalf of the church presented brother Walker (M.W.) to the Presbytery for ordination.

H.T. Smith, Mod.
J. A. Brown, Clerk

Judging from this letter, Dr. Allen was practicing medicine in 1894. His medical education could have taken place somewhere between the years 1885-1891. He would have been 18 years old in 1885 and in 1891, 24 years old.

In 1896, A.M.Allen received land (43 5/10 acres) on Spartanburg Road, Spartanburg, SC from Lindsey H. Cramer. (Spartanburg Co. Courthouse, Book of Deeds). Dr. Allen married Emily Josephine Rogers sometime between the years 1896 and 1898. In the year 1898 [Emily] "Josephine et al [sold] to J.M. Lanham-Woodruff Township - 250 acres - $10.21 (her interest 1/12 of 1/8). She was 21 years old.

Aletha Mayfield Allen, Mayfield's mother died Jan. 22. 1901. She was buried in Liberty Hill Methodist Church Cemetery- her home church. She remained at Liberty Hill even though Rev. Jesse went to Abner Creek and became a Baptist. The next year after her death (1902), Dr. Allen and his brother Henry Milton Allen petitioned the court for the sale of the 'Mayfield Homeplace' from Manora Jane Allen and Z.S. Allen and Madeline Allen. The home-place was sold to P. E. Smith. (Manora Jane was Mayfield's sister. Z.S. Allen and Madeline Allen are not known.) Wonder where Manora Jane went to live? This would be an area for research, What Ever Happened to Manora Jane?

Five years after his mother's death, Dr. Allen's wife, Josephine died (1906). He was left with three children, Harold, Ellyn and Jessica. Josephine was buried in Walnut Grove Cemetery where her mother and many Rogers' relatives are buried. Daughter

Ellyn was named for her grandmother, Nancy Llewellyn Lanham Rogers (Llewellyn changed to Ellyn).

Caroline Mae (May) Rogers, the sister of Josephine Allen, married Wade Layton who died Jan 1, 1904. A son, Hugh, was born to them. May, as she was known, married Dr. A. M. Allen (1906 0r 1907) and became stepmother to her nephew Harold and nieces Ellyn and Jessie. Her own son was not allowed to come into the home. A relative, Mrs. Rhoda Rogers provided a home for him. In 1919, D.M.Burroughs of Conway, SC.was named General Guardian to handle her son's inheritance from his grandfather Layton ($2138).

Certainly May must have missed her son but another son was born in 1907, Albert Lanham Allen and a daughter, Josephine Annie Allen in 1909. In 1911, my father, Louis George Milton Allen was born and in 1914, Marion C. Allen. Now May had her four children and three stepchildren to care for.

My father, Louis Allen, told how his father required him to learn a new word from the dictionary every day and every evening he would recite the word and its definition to his father. It is no wonder my father had such a great vocabulary!! He mentioned that he accompanied Dr. Allen in his buggy when he made house calls. My Dad, Louis G. Allen said his father's manner was entirely different with his patients and their families than at home with his own family. All the Allen siblings have confirmed Dr. Allen had a Dr. Jekyll/Mr. Hyde personality.

Louis, my father, delivered newspapers before school and after school he worked in a newspaper office in Spartanburg. He made enough money to buy his own clothes through high school. There were more real estate transactions for Dr. Allen in 1912, 1916, 1917 and 1918. Land was bought from Rosa Lee Stepp (263 20/100 acres) near Switzer Depot - C & W.C. Railroad, near Woodruff. Also he received land from brother-in-law, W.A.Rogers-[Lots] 3, and 10, near Glendale. In 1916 land was sold by Dr. Allen to Trustees of Switzer School Dist. 41; H.E. Chandler and J. Hugh Means-2 Lots Switzer, 1 Lot ben Avon. Land was bought again in 1918; from Floyd Thomas (5 8/100 acres) Glendale Road; David Thomas 1 Lot Glendale and from Julius Lucas, 1 Lot Pine St., Spartanburg, SC. The Lot on Pine St. may be the one my Dad remembered as having fireplaces in every bedroom-and being a brick house!! The family may have been living there when Dad's mother died in 1921.

When Daddy was ten years old, he was downtown at the bus station in Spartanburg. My uncle Marion, seven years old, ran to the bus station to tell him to come home-- "Mother has died...!" Uncle Marion told how well he remembered running to the bus station but my Dad couldn't remember Marion coming to get him.
My father did tell me about the time there was a fire in the home and everyone was running around hollering, "Fire, Fire", while this was going on, his mother was down beside the bed saying her prayers. He said she finished saying her prayers before getting up!! This made a memorable impression upon him. That is the only story I ever heard Daddy tell about his mother. Uncle Albert told of her being a teacher before marrying and that she taught him reading. If she taught my Dad to read, he didn't remember it.

I believe Daddy somehow shielded himself so that he wouldn't be hurt. There are times a person can go through everyday activities without seeing the details because their mind is elsewhere! I think we all have periods when we 'daydream' and probably find contentment there. Also there are individuals who can passively accept rather than struggle against the blows that assault them.

There are so many things in my life that I can't remember!! I often wonder why? Was it because it wasn't important? I don't think so. A great many of my memories are tied to music. One that comes to mind is a memory of an urgent trip to a doctor's office. My mother was having 'mini-strokes;' her eye was protruding strangely and she couldn't close her eyelid. Her mental condition was deteriorating; she was losing weight and she couldn't feed her-self. She was able to travel with help and my Dad and I were tak-ing her from Greer to Greenville, about 17 miles. We reached the Church St. bypass and passed Christ Episcopal Church; music was playing on the car radio; it seemed to reflect the sadness of the occasion:

> If I could save Time in a Bottle,
> The first thing that I'd like to do
> Is to save every day 'til eternity passes away, just to spend
> > them with you.
> If I could make days last forever,
> If words could make wishes come true,
> I'd save every day like a Treasure and
> Then again I would spend them with you
>
> If I had a box just for wishes
> And dreams that could never come true
> The box would be empty except for the memory
> Of how they were answered by you.
>
> But there never seems to be enough Time
> To do the things you want to do once you find them
> I've looked around enough to know
> That you're the one I want to go through Time With
> > Time In A Bottle
> > Words and Lyrics by Jim Croce

The doctor's diagnosis was stroke and it involved the carotid artery. The office was just across the street from Greenville General Hospital. Mama was able with our help to walk across the street and up the many steps into the hospital where she stayed and later lapsed into a coma. She did improve but gradually she lapsed into another coma from which she never returned. (Feb. 7, 1980)

Never having met grandmother, May Allen, I have to imag-ine she was like my Dad. I know what he was like and his person-ality doesn't seem like his father's. He smiled easily, was tolerant of others, enjoyed easy-listening music and whistled and hummed when he heard music he liked. In spite of his easy-going manner, he demanded your respect. He was confident of who he was but was not opinionated. In some ways he was a loner, he liked people but didn't need them all the time. You could say he was a peaceful man but he could be pushed too far and then you'd better look out!! It may appear   that he had no faults, but this is not true, he did have faults but the faults were caused by his great sensitivity and probably the insecurity in his home and early life. To those who knew him, they will know what his flaws were. Regardless, my love for him never changed and I always appreciated his sweet loving nature.

It is a fact that stress building day after day without relief can cause serious health problems. This may have been a factor in the heart attack that killed Daddy's mother. Some families have a history of heart disease. I don't know this is the case. My Dad and his brother, Uncle Albert both had heart problems. Uncle Albert died because of his heart condition. My father also had a heart attack but was saved by a traecheotomy and treated medically for it. Later he developed throat cancer. After undergoing radiation, which didn't work, he underwent throat surgery. After the throat surgery in Atlanta (Emory University Hospital) he never was able to eat. A feeding tube from his nose into his stomach was inserted and from which he received his feedings.

Even tho' this was a sad time, my Dad was never any trouble. He lived with us for seven years; the last years were the cancer years. A blood clot is what killed him. He was in his bed; I had just helped him back into it. He said. " I feel like I'm going to faint." He reached out and held on to my hand; his eyes rolled abnormally and he sighed and his mouth clamped tightly shut ! I knew he was dead and I knelt by the bed holding his hand. I knelt and prayed and stayed and talked with him for a while before I called anyone.

My Dad graduated from Spartanburg High School in 1929. By 1927/28 Dr. Allen married for the third time. He married his sister-in-law, Josie Moore Rogers. She was the widow of Rev.

Samuel Rogers (who died in 1918), the brother of Josephine and May Rogers Allen. She and Samuel had four sons and a daughter. In 1927, Dr. Allen and Josie lived on 359 S. Spring St, in Spartanburg and my dad was sixteen. Dr. Allen was sixty and Josie, fifty. The "depression of the twenties" caused Dr. Allen to lose his home on Pine St., but he sent his son, Louis to the Medical College of Charleston, in Charleston, SC. (1930). Another move, 1931, and the Allens were now on 146 Forest St., Spartanburg, SC. Certainly Dr. Allen was feeling stress as he lost almost all he had in the 20's and 30's. Louis was a college student, but he had surgery probably the summer of 1929 or 1930, for removal of his appendix at Chick Springs Hospital, Taylors, SC. The hospital is no longer there but those in the upstate knew its fame; in fact, my father wouldn't have gone to Taylors instead of Spartanburg, had there not been excellent reports about Chick Springs Hospital

My mother was in training as a nurse at Chick Springs Hospital and was one of my Dad's nurses. They eloped in 1931 and were married the 11th of August at St. Johannes Lutheran Church, in Charleston, SC. Was it my mother's idea or my father's? Both had reasons to keep the marriage a secret. My mother needed to finish nursing school and my father knew Dr. Allen wouldn't help with college expense if he married. As it turned out, Mama did quit nursing school and she joined my Dad in Charleston. They lived on Rutledge Avenue in Charleston and that's where I was born, January 20, 1933.

Upon graduation, Louis worked as a 'soda jerk'!! He couldn't find a job as a pharmacist. In 1936, he was working as a druggist at Gainey's Drug Store in Charleston. This was the year his father died. Dr. Allen wrote a letter to him asking for certain medications. He told Louis his arthritis had kept him from writing and that the cold weather made it hard for him to write. The letter is from A.M. Allen's last residence, a farm outside of Whitmire, SC. It was written March 28, 1936 and Dr. Allen died the 24th of August 1936 just five months later. His age at death was 69. Here follows the letter:

Whitmire, S.C.
Route #2
Mar. 28, 1936

Dear Louis,

Send:
100 tablets - neo-cinebophen 7 ½ grain
Eye drops

I will send check for the tablets and eye drops. If this is not enough, let me know and I will send the balance.

I received your letter some time ago but on account of the very cold weather and on account of suffering more during the cold weather, I have neglected to answer it. I am sorry you are not pleased with your work lately. I hope you like it better now.

I don't know what to advise you for every person usually knows their own business best. I hardly think we will be able to work on the farm. Besides there is absolutely nothing to farming since the boll weevil is here. Even if you should go up in Spartanburg County and cultivate your own farm.

I have no news that will interest you. Albert has recently gone to the University Medical College of North Carolina, where they have given him a scholarship for four months. I don't know what he will do at the expiration of that time. I don't suppose he knows himself. Marion will be home before long for spring holidays.

Your father,
A. M. Allen

**Dr. A. Mayfield Allen, Wife, Mae Layton Allen
and children Josephine and Albert Allen**

Josephine Allen in her later years

Louis G. Allen and Sister Ellyn Gleaton

Cousin Carolyn Gleaton, Louis Allen and Toya Allen

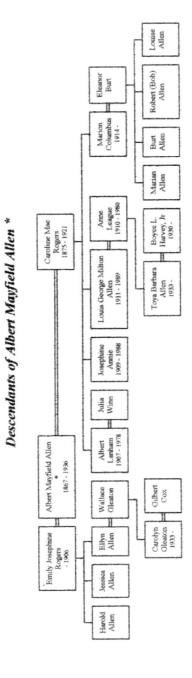

Descendants of Albert Mayfield Allen *

Chapter Fifteen
Anne, Louis and Charleston

In February of 1929, Margaret Anne League wrote the Eleventh Grade Class Poem for the Simpsonville High School Yearbook, Simpsonville, S.C.

Class Poem
Oh, brave soldiers of class '29
Our first battle's over, now college don't mind
You have fought faithfully and held 'til the last
You've brought great honor to our Senior Class.

A great field of knowledge you now do possess,
Won by striving and studying, we now must confess
You've fought faithfully, at least you tho't so,
But never give up there is much yet to know.

Now your hard studies you never must drop
Don't fail to push on and go over the top
You want to be able, a college man face
And tell him you're ready to take his own place.

Let's march onward as tho' we were classed
To a higher goal than we had in the past
We'll conquer the world with its joy and its strife
There we'll march onward to our future life.

A.L.
2/18/29

Louis G. Allen files a report as the retiring Historian of the Iota Chapter, to the Grand Historian for the year ending Feb. 15, 1931. The number of students (Medical College of Charleston) initiated into the chapter during the year were eight; the number in the chapter

**Marriage Document
for Louis Allen and Anne League**

Anne League

at the opening of the College year were six—a total of fourteen active members.

This form has Louis' signature as the Retiring Historian. His School address: Medical College of Charleston, SC. His home address: 146 Forest St., Spartanburg, SC. For all purposes, his home is now Charleston, SC. By August 11th, he and Anne League will be married.

From Simpsonville in 1929, to nurses' training at Chick Springs at Taylors (1930) to marriage and elopement (1931) and the start of Housekeeping in Charleston (1932), Anne League Allen's diaries give clues and insight into the lives of Anne, Louis and family.

Sun. Aug. 9th, 1931:	Excerpt from Anne League's diary, "Sally and I leave for Charleston; Uncle Creight's Chauffer came up for us. Got in Charleston in p.m. and had a date with Louis and Boy, Oh Boy, was my Mother's Anne crazy to see him. He looked so awfully good with light tan summer suit on"
Mon. Aug. 10th, 1931:	Louis and I are planning to marry secretly tomorrow night.
Tues Aug. 11th, 1931:	"Bought all my wedding things today. Uncle Creight gave me $25.00 and did it come in handy. So tonite at 8 o'clock Louis and I take the final steps. Oh! I've never been happier! Would you believe me when I say he brought me home at 11 o'clock? Still the virgin but now just how long this will last don't know but hope it will 'till we can live openly together.

Chapter Sixteen
Papa's Brother, Creighton League
Anne and Louis Continued
Simpsonville and Charleston again
Letter from Papa, Thomas C. League

The 1930 Census of Charleston, SC (Chicora Village) recorded Andrew C. [Creighton] League as the 56 (actually 59) year old head of the house [valued at 5000]; married for nine years to wife, Bessie Major, age 47. Also listed living in the household was Floyd Major, Bessie's brother, age 39. Uncle Creight's position was County Inspector of Sanitation. Floyd Major's position was Chauffer for the County Inspector. The column, listing whether person is a veteran, was answered yes for Creighton League and the War he served in was the Spanish-American War. According to Aunt Mays (League) Greene, he was a naval officer for twenty odd years. He died Oct. 15, 1932 in Charleston, SC.

His home in Charleston, was where Anne and her sister, Sally stayed when Anne married Louis Allen. Creight was the one who gave Anne money to buy clothes for her wedding. Sally referred to Anne and Louis in a short 10-day written account of her vacation in Charleston.

On Aug. 11th, she said: "We went to town and got new clothes. Came home and dressed. Louis came up and they [he and Anne] carried me to Boykin's (girlfriend, Boykin Wells.) We had dates, went to Folly [beach]. Boykin and I were nervous over the big affair" [Anne and Louis elopement.]

On Aug. 13th: "…. Boykin and I scared stiff going and coming about Louis and Anne. Had dates tonight and went to a show."

Sally knew something about the elopement of Anne and Louis, but even in her writing. It was a secret!

Anne and Louis Continued

Anne wrote a postcard to Louis at 181 Meeting St., in Charleston, SC; written from Chicks Springs Sanitarium: Taylors, SC. A picture of Chick Springs is on the front of the postcard and the postmark appears to be October 1931:

My Dearest,

It is 6:30 a.m. and the mail leaves at 7 o'clock so U-C- I must hurry—I worked all day yesterday, went on Spec. [duty] and worked all night last night. Just haven't had time to write at all. Will try to write tonight on duty. Here's hoping I'm not on Spec. Sat. week at night—What you say? Loads and loads of love,

Anne

Here is a copy of a letter from the SC Board of Pharmacy, Columbia, SC, dated Dec. 22, 1932, to Mr. L. G. Allen, Charleston, SC:

The South Carolina Board of Pharmacy

Dear Sir:

Replying to your letter with reference to your certificate, wish to advise that I received it all O.K. but you should know that in turn this certificate has to go the rounds to be signed by each member of the board. Just as soon as I get their signatures to it I will forward it to you.

As a rule we do not send certificates over the state to the various board members for their signatures—usually we hold them until the next meeting for fear of them being lost in the mail. However I sent yours out and as I said above, as soon as it is returned, I will forward it to you.

Very truly yours,
J. M. Atkinson, Secy.

Simpsonville Visit

As of July, 1932, L. G. and Anne were visiting with her parents, Emmie and Tom League. A letter from fellow druggist, Tom Byrd (Charleston, SC) came to Louis Allen c/o Mr. T. C. League, Rt. 1, Simpsonville, SC. Since "the depression" resulted in a lack of job opportunities, Louis may have been checking the Simpsonville/Greenville area for work. Tom Byrd says, "If you can get anything that will afford you a descent living, take it. On the other hand, if you see an opening for a good drug store, let me know at once. The only time to start is when we are young. It is my greatest ambition for you and me to get into something together so keep in close touch with me and if anything turns up, grab it."

Charleston, Again

Anne wrote from 182 Rutledge Ave., Charleston, SC, to her mother, Emmie League. The postmark is torn and is not recognizable, but it probably was written before 1936 or after 1933. I rationalize: I was born in January 1933 and Anne says, "Toya is just too rotten for words." [I was born on Rutledge Ave.] Continuing, Anne tells Emmie: "Louis said to tell you he really did enjoy being at home with you all. He said he didn't know he was having such a good time until he went down to his Daddy's—said he'd gone crazy if he had to spend a week with his Daddy. Altho' he was glad to see him." Louis' father, Dr. A.M. Allen, died in 1936; therefore, the year of this writing must have been either 1934 or 1935.

Louis wrote three letters to Anne c/o Mrs. T.C. League, Rt. #5, Greer, SC. [Note: mail at Granny's could be addressed Rt. 1, Simpsonville or Rt.5, Greer.] Emmie was sick and Anne and Toya were staying with her. Two letters were written from 17 ½ Doughty St., Charleston, SC and one, from Gainey's Drug Store in Charleston. All were dated in May 1936 [20th, 22nd and 24th.] Louis writes 12:00 a.m. May 22nd:

My Own Darling,

"Gosh but I'm tired tonight—been at it since seven this a.m. and don't care to go anymore. I tried to borrow some money tonight to send so you could buy Toya some shoes but nobody seems to have any." In letter dated may 20th: "Do you want me to get 'Possum's shoes Saturday? How is she—Boy I'd like to see her."? May 24th he says, "Well, Darling am tired and just simply hurt. So am going to turn in. Let me know the type of shoes you want her to have. How is Mama? When do you think you will come home? I do want to see you and Possum more than anything in the world and do want you to come on home but if you think you had better stay a little longer on account of your Mama, its okay. I do miss you tho' but I don't guess it isn't right for you to run off and leave her in bed. I love you more than all the world and do miss you so much. Kiss Toya for me and tell her that Daddy loves her 'most of all'...G'nite my sweet and pleasant dreams. I'll always be yours and only your very own." [Signed] L. George

Sally, Anne's sister and Herschel, Anne's brother were living with Anne and Louis in Charleston. Aunt Sally worked at the Francis Marion Hotel as a waitress and uncle Herk worked for Mr. Blanton in a plant that manufactured Guano—a type of fertilizer. In one letter, Louis says: "We are sending some cash. Herschel 10 dollars for Mama and I am doing good to send three. Our dear friend, Mr. Blanton also did us the favor by coming. First time he has been around since you left. Arnold also had a date with Sally so he was there also. (Arnold Connelly a pharmacist from Easley, SC working in Charleston .) Incidentally, he [Arnold] is quitting on the first? Asked for a certain sum of raise which was not granted so he turned in his resignation."

Emmie probably had the 'flu' when Anne was staying with her in 1936. But in 1937, she would be even more disabled in a hospital in Washington, D.C. She had a broken pelvis, among many other injuries. Helen League, Daughter-in-law (wife of Anne's brother, Tom) writes to Anne—Aug. 13, 1937.

Dear Anne,

Well, I just don't know how or where to begin—! Gee, just imagine had nothing happened, I would have been in South Carolina now!

I haven't been able to go to the hospital to see your Mother, but Tom has been going almost every night. I shall not tell you how your mother looked just after the accident—only I talked to her and she never answered—just stared at me with glassy eyes—and my heart stuck in my throat… However, she was finally taken out of the machine and rushed to the hospital—as was Chick [another daughter-in-law, wife of Anne's brother, Harry.] I followed with my baby [my cousin, Patsy League] in another car. I thought my legs were broken—however, just the muscle was torn from the bone. Today is my first day up. I didn't go to the hospital here in D.C. I came home to my Mother's home and have been ever since. My neck and shoulders were sprained—and maybe I'll have to have x-rays to determine the full injury of my leg—Here I am gabbing about myself when I know you want to hear about your Mother. She will be in the hospital, I guess for sometime, I believe you already know how badly she has been hurt—Everything is being done to make her more comfortable. Tom told me she is miserable being bandaged up the way she is, in this hot weather—gee, I can't write any more, altho' I do think it would be nice if you could come up here—You could stay with me. I have a larger place now and can put you all up—won't you come? I think your Mother would like it very much if you came—Please write to me and don't forget my new address is: 1109 Halbrook Terrace NE, Apt. 4. Please give our love to Sallie, Herk, Toya and you, of course. Please write.

Best Wishes,
Helen

Letter from Papa, Thomas C. League

Dear Anne and All,

Had letter from Ma yesterday saying she was doing fairly well. Glad to know she is still on the mend. We came from there

90

one week ago today. Dr. thought she would have at least 3 more weeks there but I doubt if she will be able to leave then, as I think she is hurt worse than they think (hope not, though,) after looking at that car don't see how some of them didn't get killed.

She was pretty blue when we got there but seemed to feel better after she found out how things were at home. Of course, they haven't been so rosy but we didn't tell her.

Think all enjoyed trip fairly well. Ed and Madge [friends, Ed and Madge Reid] got to see a good bit of D.C., as for myself, didn't go anywhere but the hospital and Tom's. Rained most of the time we were there.

We are making out fairly well—Bran [Anne's baby brother, about 16 years old] eats dinner out most every day somewhere and I eat what's left from breakfast, if any.

Am working on Franklin's car—[Franklin Smith, half brother of Emmie] trying to make a little 'jack.' Won't be much but this is one time I am going to collect.

Well, write us. You know we get lonesome and blue, too.
Love to all,
Dad

91

Chapter Seventeen
Annes's Diaries
1936, 1938

Mar. 9, 1936: Got out of bed and went to see house on Doughty Street. Decided to take it—$26.00 per month. Can't sleep tonight—am so excited about new house! Kinda hate to leave 'ole 182 Rutledge after being here almost three years.

Mar. 11, 1936: I started packing things to move. L.G. had p.m. off. We went to Picture. We spent our last night at the 'old place', which has been our 1st home, and we certainly grew to love it!

Mar. 23, 1936: Waked up this a.m. and thought I was dreaming when I saw Mama. I was so glad to see her. I could hardly believe I wasn't dreaming. Mama says Toya has whooping cough and she is real sick with temperature. Tonight Mama, Sally and Herschel went to show. L.G. and I stayed with Toya.

Mar. 24, 1936: Mama left early this a.m. Do wish she could have stayed on. Had doctor with Toya—said she had whooping cough...

Apr. 6, 1936: Had Dr. Height this a.m. Says of course I have whooping cough!

May 4, 1936: I was called on a case this p.m. A Miss Lewis about 75 years old and very sweet. She had heart attack. Tonite I'm sleeping right in the room with her.

May 5, 1936: ...this a.m. at 6 o'clock and stayed with my patient all day. Got off at 7 o'clock.

May 7, 1936: Carried Toya to hospital this a.m. and had her tonsils out. One a.m.—staying with her tonite....

[Except for a couple of entries in June 1936, the rest of the year is blank.]

Jan. 1, 1938: I awakened this a.m. with my head still spinning from the New Year's Eve party at Fountain Inn [restaurant in Charleston, SC]. Doris and Arthur [Kinser], Sally and Arnold, Louis and myself made the party. This p.m. I carried Toya to see a picture and to bed at 9. Read and read and sketched off a cartoon or two—Oh! How I would love to write or draw or paint—but can't mention it, they'd think I'd lost me whole mind.

Felt pretty good all day, except my back and sides. I should have gone to doctor but just didn't get there. I do wish I could have another child 'cause 'ole L.G. wants one so bad but 'tis nothing I can do about it....

Jan. 14, 1938: (Anne mentions working on Sally's memory book) I have been working on it since last June 1937. (Aunt Sally would marry July 25, 1937 to Arnold Connelly.)

Lessie [the colored maid] is sick and didn't come to work this p.m. So I had to get up early and cook breakfast and clean house and had it all cleaned at 9:30—Would hate to lose her. She has worked 5 years for us. L.G. and Toya went to see picture this p.m. I read a Diary of Helen Keller on her voyage to England— She is so awfully smart and brave! Makes one feel so useless. It was written just after her teacher died, Oct. 26, 1936.

[Sally and Arnold separated Feb. 7, 1938]
Feb. 8, 1938: Sally and I went around to her apartment, which seemed so lonesome and sad to her and got all her things together and packed his [Arnold's]. There's something so awfully sad in breaking up a home. This p.m. we went to show—Came home to find Mama, Louie [Anne's brother], Harry and Chick and Harry, Jr. Everyone put up a good front on account of Sally—when deep down inside our hearts simply bled for her. She is so good and sweet and has had so many roads to travel...

93

Feb. 9, 1938: We all go back around to Sally's Apartment and finish packing. It is such a beautiful apartment—5 rooms upstairs – 60 Pitt Street...Sally stayed with me tonight.

Feb. 10, 1938: ...Sally is going on to Mama's and stay till Sun, or Mon, and then is going to Washington, D. C. with Harry. Think it will be the best thing for her. They left here at 4 p.m. I hated to see them leave but when I kissed Sally 'bye, my heart felt as if some one was crushing it into tiny bits.

Feb. 22, 1938: I went again to doctor this a.m. Grandpa [D.F. Smith] was 90 years old today.

Feb. 29, 1938: ...Tonight Sally called me from D.C., at the "Mayflower Hotel"—having dinner with J. George Stewart, the congressman boyfriend she used to go with and who asked her to marry him and she refused.

Mar. 2, 1938: Sally came in early this a.m.—cold as ice! I was so glad to see her I most cried for joy. She went down to see her lawyer...

Mar. 3, 1938: Branford [Anne's baby brother] came— Awfully glad to see him.

Mar. 6, 1938: Sally, Branford, Herschel and Pate [friend] played tennis today.

Mar. 7, 1938: Lessie is off all day, so Sally, Bran and Toya went to a show this p.m.—Arnold came around for the 1st time and asked Sally if she wanted to come back to him.

Mar. 9, 1938: Branford got up early this a.m. to go home. I hate to see him go but know Mama wants him there B-4 he leaves for the Navy. I do so hope he makes good in the U.S.N and there won't be a war while he's in—The way the country is now it wouldn't surprise anyone to see war anytime.... Bran has so much good in him and I'm so proud of him and love him dearly....

Mar. 13, 1938: Sally got up early and cooked breakfast and dressed Toya for Sunday School.

Mar 23, 1938: Sally got a pair of pants and an awfully sweet card from 'Mother Connelly.'

Mar. 24, 1938: Sally went to work today at 5 o'clock at Brewton's Inn on Church Street. Toya has 'flu'. I think she had temp all last nite and couldn't sleep.

Mar. 25, 1938: I got a telegram this a.m. that Grandpa [Smith] died today. I was expecting it tho'—he was awfully sick. We want to go up but Sally has just gone to work and can't afford to be off now. Herschel and Louis can't either—He [Grandpa] was a wonderful person—First deacon of Cross Roads Baptist Church.

Mar. 26, 1938: Today is Sally's birthday. Aunt Bessie [Uncle Creight's widow] came this p.m.—Sally got a book from Arnold and a pretty birthday card—was 1st card she has ever gotten from him. I gave her a jar of 'Yardley' and Toya gave her a powder puff...

Apr. 7, 1938: [Anne and Toya are visiting her mother, Emmie League at Cross Rds.] Louis came up this p.m. Mama went with Toya and me to meet him.

Apr. 8, 1938: Louis got up early and went to Union to settle Dr. A.M.Allen's [his Daddy] estate, as he was sole executor. Got back to Mama's around 4 p.m.—Still cold and raining and is impossible for us to start back to Charleston this p.m., so L.G. wired Gainey that we would be in a.m....

Apr. 12, 1938: [Back in Charleston] Sally served tonight at the Dock Street Theater to 200 guests of whom "George Arliss" [the movie star] was guest of honor. She came home to find a letter from Arnold.

Apr. 15, 1938: Sally got a special delivery from Arnold today begging her to come to him.

Apr. 18, 1938: Mama is 52 years old today. I wrote her a long letter.

May 1, 1938: Herschel and Virginia were married early this a.m.—Much to everyone's surprise. Sally and I went to church at Citadel Square and Toya went to Sunday School at Bethel.

May 4, 1938: Arnold came this a.m. and he and Sally talked quite a while but never accomplished much—he left about noon and didn't hear any more from him. Virginia came around—Louis and I drank to newly weds.

May 5, 1938: Arnold left town without a word to anyone.

May 9, 1938: Louis had a telegram from Ellyn this a.m. that his half-brother, Hugh Layton died last nite. Herschel is moving his things out today. Surely hate to see him leave. He has been with me for 4 years. But he had to marry sometime.

May 17, 1938: I went around to Alberta's this p.m. and we sewed all p.m. I made Toya a dress. She needs several more—growing so tall—and looks wonderful to me—her hair is just below her shoulders and in curls on the end. Every day she looks more and more like L.G.

June 30, 1938: …heard President Roosevelt talk from New World's Fair in New York when he laid the corner stone of the new Federal Building—his talk was wonderful—hope the Fair will give U.S. peace.

July 1, 1938: Today is the last "Old Soldiers Reunion" being held in Gettysburg—in honor of the brave men who fought 75 years ago in Civil War—all of whom are between 92 and 96 years of age. Grandpa Smith could have gone if he hadn't died in March past…today is Louie's [brother] birthday.

Aug 23, 1938: Tonight Louis's brother, Albert Allen, M.D. came from Roxborough, N.C. with Kate Suttle from Spartanburg, SC. We went down to Gainey's to see Louis—came home and talked awhile. Albert brought us some Cognac.

Aug. 31, 1938: Albert left this a.m. and he surprised me by saying he had a wonderful time.

Sep. 28, 1938: Every one in the U. S. is in constant fear of war in Europe. If there is, will the U.S. get involved—England, France, Czechoslovakia, and Italy are to meet with Hitler in the a.m. to avoid war if possible.

Sep 29, 1938: At 8:10 this a.m. a tornado hit Charleston; killing 29 and wounding 200 and leaving 300 homeless!! It is the worst thing to happen here since the earthquake 53 years ago—no radio, no lights, no paper. Tonight everything is in total darkness.

Oct. 6, 1938: Louis has felt bad all day. Tonite had to come home from work at 10 o'clock. I called Dr. Beckman and he took him on to Baker's Hospital –with a strangulated hernia!! I went with them—he was operated on at one a.m.

Oct. 16, 1938: This is a happy day in the Allen home. Louis came home this p.m. in ambulance (5:30 p.m.)

Oct 18, 1938: Louis sat up for 1st time today. I helped him out of bed and into chair. Dr. Beckman came this p.m.

Nov. 1, 1938: We are planning going up to Mama's—don't know whether Louis can go or not.

Nov. 2, 1938: Dr. Beckman said L.G. was able to go. Insurance Co. sent notice they had refused to pay L.G.

Nov. 3, 1938: Louis, Toya and I left home for Greenville—had pleasant trip. I drove most all way and arrived at Mama's about 7:30 p.m.

Nov.29, 1938: [Back in Charleston] L.G. and I went downtown and bought maple dinette suite for $99.94—got a trade-in of $25.00 on old breakfast room suite and studio couch. I am so proud of it! Have house all cleaned now for Christmas. [Note by author: Maple dinette and china cabinet are in my dining room, still being used.]

Nov. 30, 1938: Took black paint off old 'wash stand' and painted it maple—looks like new. [I believe this is now in my granddaughter, Meryl's bedroom.]

Dec. 22, 1938: Toya went to Christmas Tree at church and then I took her down on the 'green' to hear Christmas Carols.

Dec. 24, 1938: Mom, Pop, Sally and Grady [Yeargin] came. Tonite we gave presents to all here and had a wonderful time.

Left to right: Louis & Anne Allen, Boykin Wells, Doris Kinser, Arnold Connelly, Behind Arnold: Arthur Kinser, Sally League Connelly and Virginia Shuler League, wife of Herschel League.

Chapter Eighteen
Anne's Diaries
1939 – 1940

[In Charleston, Anne writes her New Year's Resolution]
Jan. l, 1939: I resolve to forgive everyone for anything this year—to have more faith in myself and in God and will power enough to get well. And most important of all to live a better and beautiful life and to help Louis and Toya do the same.

Jan. 2, 1939: L.G. is off this a.m. and tonight—Sally is still with us—which I'm so thankful for. Sometimes I think that I am as empty as a shell when she isn't with me or near me.

Feb. 6, 1939: I feel awfully proud today. Took Toya to school this a.m. and stayed all a.m.

Feb. 21, 1939: Toya walked to store [Gainey's] today from school and was thrilled that she crossed alone. This p.m. I went to Parent-Teacher meeting at West End Dairy—came on home early and L.G. and I went to show—saw Wallace Beery in "Stand Up and Fight."

Feb. 25, 1939: Little Doris [Renken] spent day with Toya. It has rained all week and is still raining. News is still about war—pictures are about war—talk of war. I truly hope it will never be in U.S.

Feb. 26, 1939: The news on radio is all about war in Europe—am afraid the U.S. isn't out of it yet.

Mar. 9, 1939: Mama, Harry, Chick and Grady left after breakfast this a.m.—hated to see 'em leave—only wish Mama could stay awhile with me. She looks the best I've seen her in a long time—and is so beautiful. I love her more each day that passes.

99

Mar. 13, 1939: I bought Aunt Bessie's [Creight's wife] wallpaper and ran into Virginia. We took Toya to see Shirley Temple in "The Little Princess." It was a good picture—then we came by the plant to pick up Herschel and I met Louis at 6 p.m. We ate supper with them. L.G. went to work and Sally and I listened to Edna Ferber's "So Big" on the radio—starring Barbara Stanwyk. It reminded me of Mama and how truly wonderful she is to have done all she has for all the children she has. I am so proud of her.

Mar. 16, 1939: Kept Toya home from school today—her jaw is all swollen this p.m.—sure now that it is mumps!

Mar. 29, 1939: Gainey's opened up this a.m. serving breakfast and lunch with Sally in charge of it all. She seems to like it fine. Toya went back to school.

Apr. 12, 1939: Tonight L.G. and I went up to Herk and Virginia's and played bridge. L.G. looks awfully tired. I'd give anything in the world for him to get a couple of days off and rest some but there isn't a chance in a million now.

Apr. 14, 1939: President Roosevelt made his 'peace talk' to all the world—am afraid there will be war yet for the U.S.—I hope and pray we can yet have peace.

Apr. 16, 1939: Lessie took Toya to Sunday School and Sally and I went to church. We came straight back to Gainey's and Sally went to work. I waited for L.G. to get off.

Apr. 21, 1939: Little Miss Toya took it upon herself to visit a friend of hers on her way home from school.

Apr. 29, 1939: This a.m. Hitler gave his answer to President Roosevelt. He talked for 2 hours on radio—it didn't seem to U.S. that Hitler would agree to anything concerning peace for the world. Many Mothers are praying today that the U.S. will stay out of war.

May 1, 1939: Today starts another 'panic' here. The town it seems is full of Infantile Paralysis and the Health Dept. has kept it in the dark—don't know whether to keep Toya in school or take her out.

May 2, 1939: I wrote Mama that I may come up there and bring Toya till it's over here. I pray to God for guidance as to what is best. The schools haven't closed yet.

May 3, 1939: There is another case today—making it 45 cases with 4 dead. I don't know what to do or think. Toya hasn't gone back to school.

May 4, 1939:saw my doctor this p.m. and he advised me to to on up home—said they didn't know what caused it or how to treat it. We are still in the dark about it now as we were in the beginning—I've decided to go home.

May 5, 1939: L.G., Sally, Toya, Pug [friend] and I left this p.m. for Greenville.

June 19, 1939: We (Ed Reid, L.G., Toya, Mama and I) arrived in D.C. this a.m. about 11:30—pretty much shot but all together. Tonight we got the family all together for 1st time in ages.

[Back at Cross Roads]
July 19, 1939: L.G. went to Greenville and got a job at Bolt's Drug Store, starting Saturday. I am so thrilled for him.

July 26, 1939: Louie, Emma [his wife-to-be], Louis and I went to Charleston tonight after he had worked all day at Bolt's. He seems to like Bolt very well but I know he can't last very long on the hours he has. We arrived in Charleston about 12:00 a.m.

July 27, 1939: Louis stood his Civil Service exam today. We had so much to do today—we ate dinner at Gainey's and left immediately for Greenville—arrived about 11:30—Louie and Emma left for D.C. in about 5 minutes.

Aug. 9, 1939: L.G. came in early tonight to go to Columbia. I went with him. He got the job with Searle [as a drug salesman.]

Oct. 9, 1939: Toya enters Pliney School this a.m. I plan my house all day. [Anne is drawing plans for house she and L.G. will build, on land across the road from Emmie and Tom League.]

[All in all the years 1931-1939 in Charleston, SC appear to be the happiest for Anne and Louis. They both loved Charleston. I think each one was happy to start a new life in a city without any restrictions on their life style except financially.]

[The next diary entry begins in the summer of 1940. Harsh reality and disappointment are seen and felt as Anne writes.]

July 26, 1940: Got up so nervous. Put dinner on and went down in cornfield and had a good cry but when I came back to house I could hardly keep from crying—am so weak I can hardly go—will be glad when they finish my house. [Anne is feeding the carpenters who're building her house. She is disappointed because she can't handle the hot weather and the cooking. My cousins Harry League, Jr. and Patsy League are down from Washington, D.C. for the summer. All of us are at Granny's]

[Family friend, Grady Yeargin (Owner of the Batesville Cotton Gin) is building Anne's house.]

Aug 9, 1940: Grady, Ed and Roy all came back to work today—but there is so much to do.

Aug. 20, 1940: We started taking some of my things over today—each trip we made to our new house—Boy, oh Boy! Mom's house is a mess with all the shingles off the roof—men working there and at my house!

Aug 21, 1940: Chick and Sarah (Clarice League and her sister) would come this p.m. All the shingles were off the kitchen and dining room and inside on the floor. Sally was ironing. Mom and me were moving my furniture over to my house. The house has never looked worse!

Aug. 25, 1940: Toya and Patsy went to Sunday School—people came all day to see my house. Sally and I dressed and went to see her mother-in-law and then on home and to church.

Sep 1, 1940: This a.m. Tom, Helen and Patsy left for D.C.

Sep.4, 1940: I have felt so bad all day—ran a temp. – 100 degrees. One thing is sure, my health is awfully bad or I'm on the verge of a nervous breakdown…

Sept. 17, 1940: Went to see Dr. Ross—go back for metabolism test to see if I have inward goiter.

Sep. 26, 1940: This a.m. doctor gave me sentence—No smoking, No drinking—Bad heart and stomach; Bad goiter and right kidney—very strict diet. Drink fruit juices and water.

Sep. 29, 1940: Doctor said to get all the rest and quiet I could. I think my nerves are some better—I don't have those 'sinking spells' so often.

[Aunt Sally and Granny take car trip to California. They leave Oct 1st and get back Oct. 16th.]
Oct. 16, 1940: Have been worried all day about Mama and Sally but feel deep inside that nothing is wrong. Papa is worried too. He is such a wonderful person when you know him inside and understand him. We've had a lovely time keeping things going while Mom was away—. Sally and Mom came in 11o'clock p.m.

Oct 17, 1940: All we have heard today was about their trip which was wonderful I know—Papa has gone back into his shell—

I hate to see it—he has been so happy and I have loved seeing him that way.

Nov. 5, 1940: President Franklin Roosevelt was elected President of the U.S. for the 3rd time.

Nov. 20, 1940: Louis is off tonight. Mom, Toya and I went to pictures this p.m. Got word of Louie's marriage to Emma!

Back Row: Chick League, Helen League, Anne Allen, and Emmie League
Front Row: Patsy League, Toya Allen, Harry League, Jr.

Patsy League

Emmie League holding one of her babies.

Emmie League in home of her daughter Anne Allen.

105

Anne League and Sally League
Standing is Bessie Major League, wife of Creighton League

Chapter Nineteen
Five-Year-Old Anne
and Three Year Old Sally

Papa League (Thomas Coskery League) was working as a mechanic in the Charleston Navy Yard when my mother, Anne and her sister, Sally were toddlers; five and three, respectively. Uncle Herschel (Herschel League) their brother, was born there in January 1917. He was given the name Herschel for a Charleston friend and neighbor of German ancestry. The event I'm about to speak of took place before Herschel was born. As my mother (Anne) recalled, she and sister, Sally went to the Navy Yard and asked for Tom League. Papa came to see what they wanted. They told him, "You've got to come home, mama fell and broke her back!!" He rushed home to find out what had happened. Emmie seeing him, asked why was he home? She was fine! Nothing was the matter! Possibly, she was pregnant and may have lain down—whatever, her actions were misinterpreted or imagined by Sally and Anne— rather, greatly imagined by Anne and Sally!! Who was the leader, the five-year old or the three-year old?

My Cousin, Steve Connelly (Aunt Sally's son) and I were talking about our Mothers (family get-to-gether, May 3, 2003), and he made the remark that each (Anne and Sally) had an 'impish' quality! I thought how right he was—the term 'impish' descriptively captures their ability to "pull something off." This 'playful' characteristic was probably inherited from Emmie Smith League and her Smith-Gates' ancestors.

Here is a reminiscence written in 1998 of the League sisters and life in the 'old home place.' I use a quote from Anna Quindlin: "Life is made of moments, small pieces of silver amid long stretches of gravel." (Article: " Exhaust the Little Moment," Reader's Digest, Nov. 1998, Page 84.)

Pieces of Silver 'Mid Stretches of Gravel'

Where to start? I really think I'd have to start with the memory of my grandmother, beginning her day kneeling beside the bed saying her prayers. To put this into focus, imagine a cold farmhouse with only two fireplaces downstairs—one in the front bedroom and the other, the front sitting room. Usually the fireplace had smoldering ashes from the night before. At an early age, I often slept with Granny. We'd wake to the sound of an "old time" radio that was on the wall. It was a community radio—one that the neighbors could tap into. The wiring was made possible with the help of my grandfather, Thomas Coskery League—better known as Papa. The radio program came on so early that it was still dark outside. I remember hearing the hymn, "Sweet Hour of Prayer." My grandmother, Emmie, would wipe her eyes; get up from her prayers and go milk the cows—while Papa made breakfast on an old wood-burning stove. (For the benefit of my grandchildren—you will remember the room where 'Uncle Bran' had his bed—this is the room I'm speaking of; it's also the room Uncle Bran was born in.) Granny's house was destroyed by fire in 1997.

Another memory: I sometimes slept upstairs with my Aunt Sally—-a person always loving and nurturing to me. In the winter we'd warm a brick by placing it near the fireplace. Using a towel to wrap it in, once it was hot, we'd carry the brick upstairs and put it to our feet to keep warm—since there was no heat upstairs. Feeling 'special' next to Aunt Sally, I'd go to sleep while she read.

My mom and dad lived across the road in a little house that was designed and drawn up by my mother, Anne League Allen. The shutters outside the windows had an 'A" design for Allen. My mother could draw things to scale. A creative person, who did the artwork for her high school yearbook and wrote poetry; she won a prize doing the 'charleston' at the Carolina Theater in Greenville, SC. Although my Mother and Aunt Sally did not have the privileges that money brings, they knew how to 'make do.' Mama made most of their clothes. Aunt Sally did most of the cooking and

Mama, the cleaning—because in addition to Mom and Sally there were five brothers: Harry, Thomas, Louie, Herschel and Branford. Many were the never-ending chores!

Both mama and Aunt Sally were pretty and popular. They had lovely complexions and smiles. When I remember their smiles (and they always had a smile) their dimples showed. I don't know where the dimples came from— I don't remember any other family member with dimples. But they inherited a crooked little finger, which I also inherited from Granny. (Even my Uncle Bran had the crooked little finger—I could look at his hands and see Granny's hands!)

Aunt Sally's sons, Steve and David Connelly inherited artistic skills. Steve has a drafting business—how neat and skilled his work is! David, a multi-faceted person is no longer with us but I know his presence is still felt by those who love him.

Even though Mama and Aunt Sally had little in the way of material goods as they were growing up, they were given a confidence and pride in themselves that never left them. Never insecure or unsure of themselves—they were "Leagues!" Granny had a saying for almost any occasion; one of which was, "Hold your head up high, even if you die hard." I'm sure for both Aunt Sally and mama (because of serious health problems and personal crises) there were difficult times. Yet their fun-loving, wonderful personalities never suffered. No matter how ill they were, they could always find something funny to laugh about.

I miss the fun, stories and laughter that took place whenever mama, Aunt Sally and Granny were together! They would all talk at the same time and you didn't know which one to listen to. The fun was not limited to just the girls in the League family; the brothers also brought joy to family gatherings. Unfortunately the jollity was often mixed with the 'imbibing of spirits.' This tradition did not come from the Smith side of the family. Granny's father was a hard-working, religious man—a self-made man, not one to

109

indulge in idle pleasures. He gave the land for Cross Roads Baptist Church and was one of the first deacons in the church. No, the desire for 'strong drink,' probably came through Papa—the youngest boy in his family of five sisters and an older brother. His father was a medical doctor of some prominence in the community. Papa, "that gentleman-born, Tom League," was always a gentleman, even under the influence of alcohol.

The Leagues were of Scot-French lineage. My mother always proudly told how Papa's grandfather, Dr. Andrew Creighton, came over from Scotland. He kept a diary, which mama had at one time but somehow wound up in another relative's possession. We have a portrait of Papa's mother, Annie Creighton League as a little girl; also a music book which belonged to her mother, Sarah Seddon Creighton. There is a League history done by great-aunt Mays Greene, Papa's Sister. I made copies for all the children in our family—Beth Phillips, Christopher Harvey and Andrea O'Shields.

"Life is made of moments, small pieces of silver
amid long stretches of gravel."
Quoted Anna Quindlin, article "Exhaust the Little Moment";
Reader's Digest, Nov. 1998, Page 84.

Sally Connelly and sons, David and Steven Connelly

110

Chapter Twenty
We Had a Wreck

What a coincidence! The street where we have lived forty-seven years has the same name as the town of Lancaster, SC. Lancaster, SC is the city where my family and I were in a terrible automobile accident— when I was eight years old. The effects of which remained for years. For a time the name Lancaster had an unhappy association but now I think of the happiness I've known living on Lancaster Ave. here in Greer, SC
.

The Harvey's, Bill, Toya, and Beth moved onto Lancaster Ave., in 1956. Beth's brother, Chris was born in 1957 and in 1960, a sister, Andrea joined the group. This is where the children spent their childhood and teenage years. Bill and I are still here as I write—June 17, 2003. Our children are married and have their children now and their own homes .

My Mother, Anne League Allen, kept an account of the years 1941-1942. She spoke of the "head-on collision" accident in Lancaster, SC (summer 1941). The man driving the 'other' car crossed the yellow line and Daddy, Mama and I and another couple (friends of my parents) were victims of the accident! Not only were we victims but also the little boy—the son of the driver of the other car. Both cars were completely destroyed. The man had no insurance coverage and my Daddy was left without an automobile; in fact, he had to borrow a car in order to get to work. He was working then as pharmacist at Bolt's Drug Store in downtown Greenville, SC. We lived in the Cross Roads Community, on what is now Anderson Ridge Road, Greenville county, (across the road from Granny's—Emmie and Tom League).

When my mother wrote of my hospital stay in Greenville general Hospital, the reader must know because of her injury, she was not able to visit me in Greenville General. Her foot was almost severed from the leg, at the ankle. Just a small part of the ankle and foot were attached; the rest was 'dangling'. The surgery corrected this and it healed after some time; however, that leg was always much shorter.

Mama wrote: [Sunday, July 20, 1941] We had a wreck! 37 Ford ran head-on into us. I was in operating room 5:30 till 11:15 p.m. We were 6 miles out of Lancaster. Took 3 ambulances to take us to hospital. We were all unconscious. Broke mine and Toya's legs. Cut us all bad and killed the 4 yr. Old child in other car.

Monday July 21: In Hospital, Lancaster, SC. Toya and I in same room. Today has been a nightmare. They have kept us doped all day. I can hardly breathe. My chest hurts so badly—head, arm and knee had stitches. Louis; stitches on head. Toya on face.

Tues. July 22: Herschel and Virginia [Anne's brother and his wife: Herschel and Virginia League] came last nite and Virginia came to the hospital about 3 a.m. to stay with Toya. She got sick and fainted—Toya and I didn't sleep all night and nurses' gave us hypo's—Our legs hurt all nite. Tonite, Virginia is still here and I think we can sleep.

Wed. July 23: We still are suffering and Toya had her leg put in cast today. Am worried and feel awful. Toya had ether.

Thur. July 24: the people in Lancaster have really been grand to us. They've brought gifts, books, and flowers to the Hospital. They said they knew we didn't know any one there and that it wasn't our fault. Louis had to go to Greenville. He looks so bad. He is to stay with us tonight and let Virginia go back to Hotel to sleep some.

Fri. July 25: [Anne's sister, Sally League Connelly and friend, Hal Piggot] came tonite and brought Toya and me some pajamas. Toya seems to be worse today but Dr's and nurses' don't say anything about it. Said we could go home Sun. in an ambulance. I can barely raise my head. Toya is getting so nervous and restless.

Sat. July26: Louis paid $157.00 Hospital bill. Toya's temp went up. It worries me. They give her nose drops and cold caps and plenty of fruit juices.

Sun. July 27: Left Hospital. So many people came we couldn't let them in. Louis [my dad, Louis G. Allen] and Virginia sat in front of ambulance with driver and Toya and I were on cots in back. Toya started suffering the minute we got home.

Mon July 28: Virginia was awake all nite with Toya. (Took her back to Hospital. She begged to go so they could do something for her. I took her temp. it was 104 and her leg was draining. Sent for Dr. –he called ambulance and reserved room in Greenville Gen. Hospital. Her leg was infected and smelled something awful. Virginia. and Polly Ford [a friend in the Cross Roads community] went in ambulance with her.

Tue. July 29: I can just lay here and wait and pray and hope and have faith. The preacher and lots of women from the Church came this a.m. and had prayer. I am praying and have to have faith.

Wed July 30: The top pin in Toya's leg was infected. Dr. Warren white put Toya's leg straight up in a frame over her bed and cut the cast off down to where the break was—Got tea cup full of bruised blood when he took the top pin out. She is awfully sick!

Thur. July 31: Toya in Hospital—. I live for word from her. She has been awfully bad off today. Louis is so worried. I'm worried for him. He can't eat or sleep. Doesn't have a car and has to keep someone with Toya.

Fri. Aug 1: Toya suffered all day and Virginia almost gave out. Her nerves are about shot! Started crying when Toya was crying and couldn't stop. Toya is so sick. Doctor said we could smile a little today, not laugh, but smile a little. We're so thankful, oh! Father, so thankful!

Sat. Aug 2: Louis still hasn't a car—has to work—and take someone to stay with Toya at nite and someone every a.m. and worry about me here.

[Nothing written again until]

Aug 11, 1941: Toya is still in hospital. Louis and I were married 10 yrs ago today. He gave me a pink silk housecoat. I'm so thankful Toya is better. My 10th Anniversary.

[Nothing of significance until]

Oct. 20, 1941: Toya and I stayed by ourselves today. Toya is learning to walk on her crutches. I am so thankful.

Oct. 22, 1941: Mrs. Lillie [Lillie Smith, Granny's stepmother] came this p.m. and cleaned my house. Jewel Ford [sister of Polly Ford and friend to us] brought us ice cream. Toya is walking better tonite.

Oct 22, 1941: Louis came home and took Toya over to spend day with mom. Cousin Tom McKinney spent p.m. with me. Tonite Grady [Grady Yeargin, friend of family] came by. I read till L.G. {mama called daddy, L.G.} came home. Toya walked by herself on crutches.

Oct 23, 1941: We go to Dr. today. He probed in Toya's leg and twisted my ankle. We came back by the airport and watched army planes come in.

Oct 24, 1941: Virginia sent me this diary today and Toya 'jack-stones'—Tonite Malcolm Jones and Thalia [Malcolm, son of Papa's sister, Aunt Nelle League Jones and his wife Thalia Neeley Jones] came and brought 4 jars canned fruit. Grady Y. came by

–also Ed, Madge and Nina [Ed and Madge Reid and Nina Ford, friends in the community].

Oct. 25, 1941: Sun. School sent me a basket of fruit [Cross Roads Baptist]. Sally and Piggot came. Papa [Anne's father, Thomas C. League] came late tonite. Jewel Ford has been with us all day.

[Entries omitted unless they show healing progress in Anne and Toya, or give added interest to their life at this time.]

Nov. 5, 1941: Toya can put her sore leg down now and walk on crutches. I am still in bed. Can put my foot on floor awhile——

Nov. 12 ,1941: I'm beginning to walk on crutches pretty fair——-

Nov. 19, 1941: I got another piece of bone out of my leg today. Harry Sr., Harry Jr., Chick, Louie, Emma, Tom and Patsy [Anne's brothers Harry, Louie and Tom League and Harry's wife, Chick and son, Harry, Jr. and Louie's wife Emma Shafer League and Tom's daughter, Patsy League] came in at 6 a.m. Toya and I went to Doctor. Toya hasn't been doing her leg enough. Bone has to come out.

Dec. 3, 1941: L.G. took Toya and me to Doctor. Her leg doesn't bend as much as it should but mine seems fine.

Dec. 7, 1941: War was declared on U.S. by Japan. They started bombing Hawaii.

Dec 15, 1941: Took Toya to have hair washed and set. Got her a pair of shoes. Supper out and went to Deanna Durbin picture. Had a grand time.

Jan. 18, 1941: Toya and I had our Dr's appointment—some improvement. A bone came out of Toya's leg.

[Toya's entry]
Jan. 20, 1942: Today was my birthday, had good time. Got book, 2-pr socks.
and a coat. 9 years old today.

Feb. 18, 1942: Toya and I had to go to Doctor today—- Little improvement.

[Toya's entry]
I was in play late last night. I was butterfly. I sang and danced.

May 6, 1942: Toya and I went to Doctor today. He says she's still improving—Dares me to put on shoe with a heel. We went to show afterwards.

May 15, 1942: Toya's school (Pliny) was out tonite. She was awfully cute in play. One couldn't tell that her leg was at all stiff.

June 9, 1942: Toya started taking piano lessons today (Vera Lane Verdin, teacher). Spent day with Ebb Ford [a close friend of Anne's]. We made her a baby mattress and fixed up baby bed and ironed. She is expecting soon now.

July 20, 1942: Year ago today, we had wreck. L.G., Toya, Patsy and I took Mae Renken and Doris to the train in Spartanburg, SC. [The Renkens were friends who were visiting from Charleston.]

Patsy League, Harry League Jr. and Toya Allen

Patsy, Harry and Toya with Betty Green, girl in front

Uncle Louie League and baby daughter Jerry League, 'lil' Harry, dog Shot, Toya Allen and Patsy League with dog Missy

Class picture of students from Pliney School
My friend Thelma Cooper is on the far right.
I am third from the right (Toya Allen). My friend, Thursa
Hawkins is 4th from right. Next is my 3rd cousin, Nancy
Beason; next down, Ann Snow. The next girl, can't be named.
The far left young man is John Phillips - he's the uncle of my
son-in-law David Phillips. The teacher was Mrs. Reeves.

Chapter Twenty-One
Sling the Biscuit

Are there any simple childhood games or activities from your younger days that stay with you for life—activities that made life fun? I wonder if in my memory, these events were really that wonderful? It may be that life is seen as more golden because of the innocence associated in childhood play.

Along with play, other pleasurable day-to-day happenings appear to us with the message, "Wasn't that special?" Riding a School Bus through the countryside surrounding Pliny School was such an adventure for me! My cousins, Patsy League, and Harry League, Jr., rode also. We were the last to get off (at our destination which was Granny's house, just above Cross Roads Baptist Church) thus, enabling us to take the 'grand-tour.' My cousins were not brother and sister; they were 'only children' as I was. Patsy was four years younger than I and Harry Jr. was five years older than I. At the time, it was like having a brother and sister. Their homes were in Washington, D. C. but they often stayed with Granny. When they didn't stay for the school year, they sometimes stayed for the summer. What an unexpected gift for me!!

Even though I lived across the road from Granny's, we were all usually together at Granny's. Some of the fun things we did were: working puzzles; playing with Papa's birddog, Shot; swinging in Papa's swing; petting the kittens (always there were kittens) and lying in the hammock. We played so well together—no discord or problems   I appreciate that happy time!

Harry Jr. would tell me stories of books or movies he'd seen. Storytime was upstairs after we were ready for bed. The two large bedrooms had an adjoining door. We'd open the door and lie on either side of the door because we weren't in the same bedroom. Stretched out on the floor with our heads at the door, I heard the story of "The Thirteen Steps" and "The Three Feathers." My memory is not too clear but the picture is in my mind and it seems that I was nine and Harry was thirteen or fourteen.

Patsy and I would dress up in 'old clothes' and put on 'production numbers' for the adults to watch. I think it was Patsy who sang with me, Pistol Packing Mama from the roof of the chicken coop. Harry let me ride with him on his bike to our neighbors. We waded in the creek—just down the pasture at the edge of the woods. We had 'play-like' (pronounced plike) funerals in the pasture when one of the cats died. Patsy and I once climbed out the upstairs bedroom window and sat out on the roof over the front porch. This was just before I was baptized and I remember us singing, "O Happy Day".

Family and friends sat on the porch and rocked and chatted while the children played in the front yard. It was especially nice on summer evenings with the fireflies flitting about. Dusk was a magical time with stars popping out all over the sky. One of our favorite games was "Sling the Biscuit." Today this game might be called "Statues". Each person was pulled or 'slung' by another's hand into a quick stop and had to hold the position like a statue, while the next one (the biscuit) was slung. We played this often. When we tired, we turned cartwheels all over the yard. I was the champion cart wheeler! If it was not too late, we'd draw squares in the dirt to play 'hopscotch', a game I never grew tired of playing. My good friend, Thursa Hawkins and I often played this near Papa's Horseshoe Stakes to the side of the porch.

Living out in the country was rewarding in many ways. There was so much freedom—no territorial boundaries—no neighbor's yard to stay out of—just barbed wire to keep the cows in.

Chapter Twenty-Two
From Cross Roads to Greer

The years from 1943 and 1947 presented more physical and mental crises for Anne. Returning from a 4-H Camp in the summer of 1943, I was met at the 'pick-up' site, McPherson Park, Greenville, SC, by a neighbor, Rob Ford. He told me my mother was in Greenville General Hospital—that she was sick. While I was away at camp, she had a 'nervous' breakdown. It was necessary for her to be 'institutionalized' for a short time. I never knew what happened but I think Granny knew. By September all was well again and I started back to school in the fourth grade at Pliney.

We were living in Greer when 1947 rolled around. Daddy rented out the house in the country and bought a new home (201 Church St., Greer, SC.) Our house was directly across the street from the School Superintendent, Mr. R. L. Stuart, his wife and daughter, Sara. Davenport High School was just above and to the left of the superintendent's house. I could walk across to my seventh grade class at Davenport.

How different things were at that time! Our teacher, Mrs. Stroud called the role each day and we had to answer with a Bible verse. Each row had a monitor who checked to see if all the hands and fingernails were clean! If there were any disciplinary problems, Mrs. Stroud could handle them with the leather strap she had! She didn't mind referring to someone as a 'scalawag' if he or she didn't meet her approval. She certainly didn't worry about what the parents thought!!! She was there to <u>teach</u> and there had better not be any interference! How nice it would be if the students of today could be as respectful as we were. I'm sure my daughter; Beth Phillips (1st Grade teacher at Chandler Creek Elementary School, Greer, SC) would be appreciative if all her students knew the meaning of <u>respect</u>! However, I believe before the student finishes the year, each will begin to know the meaning! It seems our society doesn't put much value on respect for anything or anyone unless the parent instills it in the home or the teacher instills it in the classroom. Can you think of any examples where respect is shown today? I think one good example is the military! Military men have respect for their officers and their Commander-in-Chief.

The move to Greer brought an insecurity that I had not felt before—not in Cross Roads Community, nor in Pliney School or in Cross Roads Baptist Church. I think of the confidence I had during my 'school days' at Pliney. Life was simple in the country. You didn't need to keep up appearances. Granny wasn't across the road and I became aware that our life was not so wholesome after all— Daddy worked all the time and Mama wasn't well.

I had some very good friends—especially Pat Golden, Dot Mason and Barbara Smith. We'd spend the night with each other; go to the movies or to some event at school. Pat and I took piano lessons from Mrs. R. B. Taylor. I'd walk down to her studio twice a week. It was in the "old Robinson Home" on South Main St. Pat and I played piano duets together. Sometimes when Dot had me over, we'd go with her family to the Greer Football Game. Barbara would ask me over on the weekend and invite me to go to church (1st Presbyterian of Greer.) The Choir Director, Miss Mary Dell Stewart asked us to join the choir—I thought that was pretty important for two seventh graders! It was fun being in the choir and Miss Mary Dell selected good music!! With Mary Dell's musical judgment and "Lib" Smith's excellent organ accompaniment, it was a joy to be a part of the music!

Miss Mary Dell was the music teacher at Central Elementary when I was in the fifth or sixth grade. Knowing I was a piano student, she asked me to play for the music class and I played, "Blue Butterflies."

My mother became ill and was in bed for a good part of the time; prior to and during the time I was in the seventh grade. She was seeing a doctor but couldn't seem to improve. Finally we went to Granny's and stayed. Daddy and I went back and forth, he to work and I to school—that way someone could be with Mama. After some days, Granny called for us: "Come, quick. I can't wake Anne up!" When we arrived, the ambulance was there waiting to take Mama to Greenville General Hospital. She was in a coma!

Mama almost died from uremic poisoning! She was in a coma for three days. I remember praying she would come out of it. Hospitalized for a month, she decided to go to Washington, D.C. to recuperate and visit her brothers, Harry, Tom and Louie. It took some time for Mom to 'come back' to herself, but this was just one more 'hurdle' Anne had overcome.

**Anne Allen and
her sister-in-law
Virginia Schuler League**

Nurse and patient, Anne Allen

Chapter Twenty-Three
Two Doctors of Note

Two doctors of importance in the Greer and Greenville areas were Dr. M. L. Peeples of Greer and Dr. George R. Wilkinson, Jr. of Greenville. In November of 1948, Dr. Wilkinson writes from the Wilkinson Clinic, Greenville, SC to Dr. M.L. Peeples:

> Dr. M. L. Peeples   Re: Mrs. Allen
> Greer, SC
>
> Thanks for letting me see Mrs. Allen again. Her condition is certainly vastly improved over what it has been before, particularly with regard to the liver status. The principal findings at this time are enclosed on a separate sheet.

On the separate sheet Dr. Wilkinson states that Mrs. L. G. Allen is 38 years of age, her height is 66" and weight is 135 1/2 pounds. The summary of findings cover five
Areas: Liver Status, Renal Status, Hypochromic Anemia, Chronic Paranasal Sinus Distress and Heart Status.

Discussion, and Treatment Suggestions:

> The electrocardiographic findings, I think, are a residuum of what has gone on before, and do not represent any new pathology.
>
> On the whole, I think the patient has tremendously improved, and should continue on the high protein, low animal fat diet.
>
> With regard to the choline chloride, one teaspoonful daily should be Sufficient.

Nibesol, one capsule after breakfast and one after dinner; and after the evening meal, Sulbegama.

An occasional shot of liver extract would probably help in getting the hemoglobin up.

It would be well for Mrs. Allen to push the proteins a little. Perhaps she is taking as much now as she can get by with.

With regard to the sinus affair, I believe it would be well for her to avoid exposure to the wind as much as possible, and keep her face warm. Some of the antihistamine drugs may be helpful; small doses of Thephorin, 25-mg. Two or three times a day as needed. Locally some Privine jelly at times in the nostrils will help, and hot applications over the face.

Rest is still essential, but I think she is able to do pretty much what she has been doing, just so she gets some rest in between times, and stays warm.

With regard to the pyelonephritis, if she has any more attacks, would suggest getting the urine alkaline with potassium citrate, one ounce; tincture of belladonna, one-half ounce; tincture of hyoscyamus, one-half ounce; aqua ad q.s. ounces six: one teaspoonful three times a day and at bedtime for a period of, say, twenty-four hours, and then Streptomycin, one-fourth gram, six doses a day for two days. Keeping the urine quite alkaline while this is being used.

After Dr. M.L. Peeples retired, Dr. Wilkinson was my mother's internist from 1947 until 1980—thirty-three years. A friend as well as a doctor, Dr. Wilkinson was the attending physician when Annie (the name he called her) died.

Dr. M. L. Peeples was remembered in an article from The Greer Citizen, entitled, Area Residents remember Dr. Marion L. Peeples, Jr.;

Dr. Peeples practiced medicine in Greer for over 30 years until his healthforced him into an early retirement in June of 1955.......

Dr. Peeples occupied the office above the old Frierson's Drug Store on Trade St. for a number of years. One pharmacist who filled many prescriptions for Dr. Peeples' patients and was one of the doctor's patients himself is Louis Allen. Allen, who lives in Greer, fondly recalls working with the physician. "He loved to laugh. He was a fine doctor and a great gentleman. I'm proud that I knew him. We thought the world of him." (Dr. Peeples died at the age of 84 in the Medial Univerity of South Carolina.)

Dr. Peeples was always available to treat a patient. "My wife had a number of ailments, and I could call him at any time of the night. He was one of those 'good-bedside-manners' doctors. I wish there were more doctors like him. I enjoyed working with him. It was always a joy to see him. I visited him some in Bluffton, (S.C.) after he moved," says Allen.

One patient who became a patient of Dr. Peeples at the age of 15 and remained one until his retirement is Mrs. Minnie Waters. She recalls her first encounter with the doctor. " My whole family was in bed with the flu, so Dr. Peeples came to see us. He went back to the drug store and got someone to bring the medicine out to us. He was our doctor from that day on...."

...She also remembers being able to call the doctor at any hour. "At night, if anyone got sick, they could go to the doctor's house. He would check them and then call Dr.

Louis Allen, so he would come and open up the drug store and fix the medicine. No one had to go to the emergency room."

As far as payment was concerned, Mrs. Waters says, "Office visits were $2. If you had it, okay, if not, it was still okay. He never asked for money as far as I know. He never sent out a bill."

**Bill Harvey (on left) and Louis Allen (on right)
in 'Old' Frierson's Drug Store**

Chapter Twenty-Four
Autograph Book

Anne collected signatures in an autograph book. She did this when she was in the hospital; when she was in Washington, D.C. (visiting her brother, Harry), and also when she was at home in Greer, SC.

A few of these autographs have been selected and cover the years 1947, 1948 and 1967:

[No date] "Here's to more red corpuscles, vein vigor and vitality."

G. R. Wilkinson

Nov. 4, 1947: "My, my, Gal! I thought I could eat, but believe to my soul, you take the cake."

Harry C. League

Nov. 11, 1947: "Here's to a girl with plenty of courage and a will to take it!"

Max Silverman, D.D.S.

Dec. 16, 1947: "Congratulations on the wonderful way you have 'come-back.'"

M. L. Peeples, Jr. M.D.

[No date] "I hope Mrs. Allen, that someday I will learn to face life without self-pity—and with courage as you do.

Nita Baswell
[Renter in Apartment with the Allen's]

Mar 13, 1967: "To the toughest white woman I've ever seen. May she always continue to 'come back.'"

Geo. Wilkinson, Jr., M.D.

**League Family
Left to Right: Anne Allen, Louie League, Sally Connelly, Harry League, T.C. League (Papa), Thomas League, Emmie League (Granny) and Herschel League**

**League Family
Standing: Herschel, Papa (T.C. League), Branford, Granny (Emmie League), Tom and Louie. Kneeling: Anne, Harry, David Connelly, and Sally.**

Chapter Twenty-Five
The Druggist's Wife

I'd say it means a lonely life

To be the corner druggist's wife,

Condemned through all the year before

To make a home above the store,

On holidays to hear him say:

"My dear the clerk is off today!

If I should order him to work,

I'd have to seek another clerk,

And clerks today of any kind

I'm sure you know are hard to find"

Time was at very early age,

I took a druggist's trivial wage

And washed the glasses and the spoons,

The bottles and the brass spittoons,

I folded all the morning through

The Seidlitz powders, white and blue,

From eight a.m. to ten at night

I heard the druggist's clerk recite

The cares, the troubles and the woes

Which endlessly the druggist knows.

Yet though they burn the midnight oil

And seven days a week must toil,

Though pharmacists are never known

On holidays and Sundays too,

When druggists would a-wooing go,

The women never answer "No."

Although it means a lonely life,

The druggist always finds a wife.

Author Unknown

It was a lonely life for Anne who truly was a 'people person.' Many times she wanted to go places and do things!! She managed somehow to see people, family and friends, until her health and accidents prevented her from driving. She had little to look forward to except family visits and working with her flowers. She enjoyed planting geraniums and coleus and begonias. A faithful maid, Millie took Mama to see her cousins and for short errands. Mama taught Millie how to drive. A friend to the family, Millie was a blessing for Mama and Daddy—also to our children, Bill and me. The children loved her and so did we. An excellent cook, we enjoyed the meals she prepared, especially her 'ham pie,' (isn't that right, Chris?)

Millie's nerves reached a breaking point when Anne, always eccentric, became more so. It was a sad day for all when Millie left. She later came to help me when Mama stayed with me [three months before she died.] I asked Millie to feed Mama because it hurt me to look at her—her vacant stare and 'bulging eye'—the result of stroke damage to her carotid artery! I knew Mama had already 'crossed over' into another world. She asked me one time, "Do you know where Toya is? I can't find her." Many caregivers can relate to this. God only knows the heartache shared by caregivers!

I think how much Anne went through in her life—beginning as a baby with diphtheria who had ten shots of antitoxin (five in each shoulder.) All of her physical and mental suffering has not been told—suffice it to say, she never was well.

Daddy and I decided to have the marker for the burial site engraved as follows:

"He who endures is more that a conqueror."

Anne and Louis Allen in front of their house in the country

Chapter Twenty-six
Goodbye, Aunt Sally

Three of my Mother's siblings were involved in World War II—Aunt Sally; the Spars, Uncle Herschel; the Seabees, and Uncle Bran; the Navy. Branford League was en route to Pearl Harbor and reached there one day after Pearl Harbor was bombed by the Japanese (Dec. 7, 1941.)

I'm not sure of the exact year in which Aunt Sally and Uncle Herk entered the service but Branford was already a sailor when war was declared with Japan. Granny received letters from all of them during the war. One of these letters was from Sally, written on "Spars" stationery—the envelope is lost and the date is not on the letter. This letter is important because Sally is about to make a change in her life—one that will make a difference for the rest of her life:

Dearest Mom and all:

Do hope all of you are all right—Can't hear a word—I'm terribly sorry that I couldn't make it for Thanksgiving but seemed as if it couldn't be helped. Do hope you had a nice one.

Grab a seat and maybe get an aspirin—for the news I'm gonna spring. Arnold came by last Friday and left yesterday morning. We patched it up and I'm going back with him as soon as I can—in fact, we had the papers drawn up and separation cancelled while he was here. I thought about it in every possible way know that it is best. He was honorably discharged from the Navy, due to physical disability obtained in actions overseas. He has quite a case of Malaria but looked wonderful. He has changed an awful lot; in lots of ways—but you'll figure that out when you see him because he'll be down to see you pretty soon—said he would like to spend a few days there with you.

133

I wrote Grady and am just hoping and praying that he'll understand. Try to help him, because I don't think, in fact I know it could never have been different as much as I would have liked for it to have been.

I had a sweet letter from Herschel and I must write him. He'll make it all right but it'll be hard at first.

This is enough I guess for one time. Write me soon and know that I love all of you dearly.

Guess it must have been meant to be this way or else I don't think it would have happened after all this time.

> Gobs and gobs of love always
> Your own gal, Sally

The precise date Sally left the service is unknown to me but she and Arnold were living in Greenwood, South Carolina, in 1944. I can verify this because I visited them and while there, Aunt Sally and I went to "open" church to pray. All the churches were opened for people to come in and pray at any time, for the U.S. military men and the Invasion of Normandy. This was known as D-Day, June 6, 1944.

In a later move, Sally and Arnold were in Newberry, S. C. and this is where their first son, Steven was born. Another son, David was born in Greenville, S.C.

Sally had serious health problems and in 1967 she was a patient in the Veteran's Hospital in Columbia, S.C. She writes from Ward #4:

Dearest Mom:

Seems as if I'm back in service—They should know a great deal about me when they get through. I'm still having tests made. Every thing and everyone here is nice. They're giving me some medication but for what I don't know as yet.

I've gotten a lot of nice cards and appreciated the letters from Chick and Virginia.

Guess Tom and Helen will be down Friday—It sure would be nice if you could go to Fla. with them.

I'm making out all right so don't worry about me. Say hello to all, and

> Much love,
> Sally

I will not mention other hospitalizations for Sally, except the one in which, she and Mama were in the same hospital at the same time—February 1980 (Greenville General.) Aunt Sally was receiving treatment for a kidney problem. Because of a previous surgery, one of her kidneys had stopped functioning and she was having pain and infection in her 'good' kidney.

Aunt Sally's room was on one of the lower floors and Mama's; on one of the upper floors. On Feb. 7, my Mother died. I went down to see Aunt Sally and to tell her. She knew (and so did her son, Steve) that Mama wasn't doing very well—I don't think she was too surprised, but still, she was hurt and upset.

After Arnold died, and Steve and David married, Sally lived alone. She managed extremely well until the last months before she died. She knew she couldn't last much longer when she told me, "I think I'm on my last leg!"

Before the last months, I'd go over and we'd go out to lunch. I spent time visiting her—meaningful, quality time.

Sometime we went to a movie or ran errands or watched TV. But gradually, she wasn't able to get out any more. She'd make a list when she needed something, and I'd get her groceries. She and I loved to read. We'd swap books; talk about the books; and on occasion I went to the library for her.

Before she was confined to her home, we often went to the S & S Cafeteria, in Greenville, SC. She especially liked the egg custard pie served there. I have this mental picture of a sunny day; walking with her to the entrance of the cafeteria—her arm is around my shoulder, saying affectionately if not verbally: We're bonded aren't we? You have my love. This is a silver moment!

Of course, in the League family, we always greeted each other with a hug and a kiss and we'd do the same when we said goodbye. Visiting Granny and Papa, we'd always kiss hello and goodbye. I'm grateful that I was a part of that warmth, and hope this tradition will continue on through our children's children.

I told a friend, "I don't know what I'll do when Aunt Sally dies!" I meant, I just didn't know how I could face it! Yet, we have to. And so it came. She died in surgery—but she was already dying before the surgery. I asked to see her and the nurse took me down to where she was—to a room near the O.R. I was able to spend some time with her. She was still warm. Even in my grief, it was a comfort to be near her. I didn't want to say goodbye.

Toya Allen and Sally League Connelly on stoop of Anne and Louis's house

Chapter-Twenty-Seven
"Toya"

For many years, my name 'toya' brought me attention. A movie, The Hatchet Man, (Edward G. Robinson and Loretta Young) is the source for my name. My mother was pregnant with me when she saw this movie (Charleston, SC). The story was about a Chinese family whose daughter was named Toya (Loretta Young.) For some reason, the name fascinated my mother—I don't know if it was supposed to have a meaning or not—whatever the reason, Toya was to be my name. Not until the late 60's did I hear of anyone, other than myself, named Toya. Now I am privileged to have a granddaughter as my namesake—Toya O'Shields.

I had not considered writing this book as my biography. Those who know me will agree that I don't relish 'being in the lime-light.' Life sometimes draws us into a spot-light whether we like it or not. Once I finished writing the story of 'Louis and Anne in Charleston,' I entered the scene with my birth, January 20, 1933 (Rutledge Avenue, Charleston, SC) and the many references to me in the chapters, 'Anne's Diaries.'

In case you (my reader) missed some of these facts, I will summarize what was covered about my early life. After entering first grade in Charleston and nearing the end of first grade, a polio epidemic hit Charleston. It caused such concern that my mother took me out of school and we came to the upstate to the Batesville Community—specifically, Cross Roads (Anderson Ridge Road today) out from Greer. We lived with my grandmother and grandfather, Emmie and Tom League. Daddy took a job with Bolt's Drug store in Greenville, SC. I went to Pliney School which was not far from Cross Roads, in fact it could be walked and I did, once or twice but I'd say it was about 3 miles. I was baptized at Cross Roads Baptist Church just down the road from Granny's. Our house was built across the road from Granny's in the 1940's. 'Anne's Diaries 1936-1938 and

1940-1941' tell even more about my early life and our family.

I remember very little about first grade, but I remember well the music we marched to in our classroom. Sensitivity to music and its message always has always been a great part of my personality. The occasional references to a work of music, such as a hymn or song have allowed me to share something of myself as I attempt to express the deep-felt emotion that is stirred within me from hearing the music and the words.

I began teaching piano some thirty years ago to help with my college tuition (remember I was a mother with three children in school when I began my college years.) In fact, I paid for my entire college expenses by teaching piano. After teaching for awhile, I began to realize I was doing exactly what God wanted me to do. The thought would come to me, "I'm exactly where I'm supposed to be."

Those college years were not easy years, for me or for my family. I went to classes in the morning and after getting the children from school (Chris and Andrea)—Beth walked to her grandmother Allen's— I taught piano in the afternoon. I had to wait until the weekend to do our family wash—then it took almost all weekend. In addition to the necessary study for courses, the piano practice (two hours every day) was necessary. But I never carried a full load—that is, never more than three courses plus piano and music courses. Naturally, as a piano major, "center stage" was another requirement. There were weekly repertoire classes in which to perform in the concert hall. You learn very quickly there will always be someone who plays better than you. Nevertheless, I managed to handle my stage-fright and successfully performed my junior and senior recitals. I'm proud of what I accomplished, but I never loved performing as I did teaching.

I thoroughly enjoyed teaching and loved my students (whether they knew it or not.) To me, a lesson was an opportunity to open up a 'whole new realm of musical mystery,' and to be a part of this learning experience was ever so rewarding! The gift of music has brought such pleasure to me throughout my life!

**Anne Allen on Doughty St.
in Charleston, CS**

**Anne, Louis and Toya Allen
in the country - probably
Woodruff Rd. Area,
Greenville County today**

**Toya Harvey at piano in Mission Church,
Redeemer Lutheran Church's first home in Greer, SC**

BOB JONES *University*
UNDERGRADUATE RECITAL SERIES 1969-70

TOYA HARVEY

Pianist

I

Sonata in B-Flat, K. 333 . . . . Mozart
 Allegro
 Andante cantabile
 Allegretto grazioso

II

Papillons, Opus 2 . . . . Schumann

III

Toccata from *Le Tombeau de Couperin* . . . . Ravel

Mrs. Harvey's recital is presented in partial fulfillment of the
requirements for the bachelor of arts degree in piano and was
prepared under the direction of Laurence Morton of the Department of Piano of the School of Fine Arts.

USHERS

Andrea Harvey Christopher Harvey Jan Morris Kathy Nelson

CONCERT CENTER

Recital Program
April 10, 1970

5:00 P.M.

140

Chapter Twenty-Eight
"Billy"

My husband, known as Billy to his family, was born February 13, 1930 in Durham, North Carolina. His father (Boyce Sr.,) was a construction worker involved in the building of Duke University. Bill's mother, Lillian Lister made these entries in Billy's Baby Book:

Born: Thursday, 55 minutes past two o'clock

Weight: 7 pounds 8 oz.

First Outing: Mother, Sister [Betty] and Mrs.Williamson carried Billy for a walk. We didn't go far, as the wind was blowing and Mother was still weak.

Seven months: Billy could sit up and crawl.

Eight months: Billy took his first steps, October 23, 1930. Also, waved bye-bye.

First Words: Daddy

First Baby Tooth: On November 14, 1930, first baby tooth peeped through.

First Christmas Gifts: wagon, bear, ball, bib, stockings, drum and fruits.

First Easter: Daddy bought sister [Betty] and Billy a pretty basket of chickens and eggs. Mother dyed some eggs but Billy was too small to play with them.

Lock of Baby Hair: between pages 26 and 27.

Family Tree: Harvey and Lister—his parents: John D. and Ella Burns

Lister— Her parents: Walton and Lennie Wilson Lister.

Billy's family returned to Greer but his father continued to work on different contruction jobs out of town. A baby sister, Peggy Jean was born August 29, 1932. For some time, the family lived with the Harvey grandparents. At some point, a move was made to Bennett Street in Greer. When the children were old enough, Lillian went to work at Victor Mill. For many years, while she worked the night shift, the children stayed by themselves. This put some responsibility on each but the most responsibility was shouldered by Betty, the oldest.

Billy went to Victor Elementary School and in the 40's he received a certificate for bringing in the most 'scrap metal'—this was during the war years (WWII) and saving scrap metal was a patriotic endeavor. Billy was a good student in elementary and in Greer High School. Not only was he a good student; but also a good son.

Bill (Billy) often spoke of what a hard worker his grandfather John D. Harvey was.—how he would 'wear him out' on the other end of a 'cross- saw' as they cut down brush and logs. The land farmed by Mr. Harvey reached a large distance across highway 101 in the area known as 'Harvey Road.' Bill rode with his grandfather when he took corn to have it ground into cornmeal.

High school friends and buddies, Sarrell Strange, James H. Hairston, 'Deacon' Jones and Denny Owens spent time with Bill at his home, spending the night and enjoying Bill's mother's cooking. Sometimes they would take weekend trips together; Georgia, Florida and Charleston.

One summer Bill worked with his dad in Florence, SC, building a bridge over a swampy area. The work was hard, but Bill stuck it out in spite of the heat and mosquitoes. After their work was finished, Bill wanted to buy a watch with his money. His daddy said: " You've got a champagne mind and a beer pocket book." Boyce L., Sr. (also called Bill) referred to Lillian his wife as "that high stepping mama."

Bill's dad had diabetes,an ailment common to many Harvey relatives. A stroke partially paralyzed one arm which he kept in a sling. He loved baseball and wrestling. I'm sure being inactive was not natural to his nature.

When Bill was seventeen he joined the National Guard and he remained a Guardsman every year (except one) until he retired at age 62 as Unit Administrator for the 178th Field Artillery Battalion Battery at Inman, SC.

The Harvey ancestral lines have not been researched in depth except for the family trees included within my book. More research needs to be done.

Billy, Jean and Betty Harvey

Chapter Twenty-Nine
Toya and Bill 1950-51

In the summer of 1950, I visited with my Uncle Harry League, in Washington, D.C. My Daddy's sister, Jessie Allen—who worked for the government's printing department—came over and arranged to take me to New York City for a weekend. It was an exceptional weekend! We rode the carriage in Central Park; shopped on 5th Avenue, stayed in the Hilton Hotel and saw the Broadway Show, Where's Charlie, with Ray Bolger. I loved it!

My Aunt, whom I had never met before, decided to call me Barbara (apparently she didn't like Toya.) But she was very nice. I was seventeen and needed time away from a teenage infatuation, which fortunately ended in a couple of years. I am grateful to my Dad for the part he and Mama played and for the support they gave me during this unhappy time!

I'm sure my Dad reimbursed Aunt Jessica for the money she spent on our trip. He probably thought of it as an investment in my future—and I think it was. It was a turn-around from one direction (one that would have made my life miserable) to another (that would bring happiness, satisfaction and fulfillment.)

The fall of 1950, I was working at Frierson's (where my Dad was pharmacist) across the street from Smith and James where Bill Harvey (my future husband) worked as salesman and bookkeeper.

Bill and I started dating in October of 1950 and by Christmas we were making plans to marry. I finished High School and we married June 26, 1951 at the First Presbyterian Church of Greer, by Reverend John K. Johnston. His daughter was my maid of honor. Preacher Johnston proved to be another great influence in my life. I'm so glad he married us and baptized our children,

Beth, Chris and Andrea! He was a man of God who truly cared for his 'flock.

It's appropriate, at this time, to tell of an Evening Service at the 1st Presbyterian Church of Greer, shortly after our marriage (1951). Bill was a member of the South Carolina National Guard and the men from the Greer unit of the 178th Field Artillery Battalion came as a group to the service. I was a choir member and was in the choir 'loft' facing the balcony and I could see all the uniformed men sitting there. Rev. Johnston had the Guardsmen sing a couple of verses of <u>Stand up, Stand up for Jesus,</u> then everyone joined in on the other verses.

How proud I was—seeing my husband and the other guardsmen in their uniforms; experiencing the music and the message; and hearing the manly voices ring out! I was filled with patriotic and religious emotion! God gives us inspiring, uplifting experiences to reach the 'inner' core of our being—to reach into our hearts!

Stand Up, Stand up for Jesus

Stand up; stand up for Jesus, ye Soldiers of the Cross,
Lift high His Royal Banner; It must not suffer Loss;
From Victory unto Victory, His Army He shall lead,
Till Every Foe is Vanquished, and Christ is Lord indeed.

Stand up, stand up for Jesus, the Trumpet call obey,
Forth to the mighty conflict, In this His Glorious Day;
Ye that are men now serve Him against unnumbered foes;
Let Courage Rise with Danger, and Strength to Strength oppose.

Stand up, stand up for Jesus, stand in His strength along;
The arm of flesh will fail you, ye dare not trust your own;
Put on the Gospel Armor, Each piece put on with prayer;
Where duty calls or danger, Be never wanting there.

Stand up, stand up for Jesus, The strife will not be long'
This day the noise of battle, The next the Victor's Song;
To him that overcometh, A crown of life shall be,
He with the King of Glory, Shall reign eternally.

Lyrics: George Duffield, 1858   Music: George J. Wells 1837

**Bill returning to Greer, SC after summer encampment with
the National Guard and Toya meeting him at the train station**

Chapter Thirty
Lancaster Avenue

Lancaster Avenue gets its name from the Lancaster family (Nannie B. Lancaster and J.B. Lancaster, Sr) who lived in the corner house at the beginning of the 2nd block of Lancaster Avenue. A dwelling owned by W. E. Harvey and family now occupies the land. The Lancaster Apartments are directly beside it. When we bought our lot, it was the last area of vacant land on our block.

We bought our lot from Mr. B.B. Cox and wife, Leona Cox. At the time Mr. Cox bought the land—17th day of March 1945, he had it recorded at the Register of Mesne Conveyance, Greenville, South Carolina. His and Mrs. Cox's home faced West Pointsett St. and the back of their house faced our lot on Lancaster, because the lots joined at the back. As I write, I must tell you that Mrs. Cox will be 104 years old this October, 2003!! She lived alone (after Mr. Cox died) until last year, 2002. Because of a fall, which resulted in a broken shoulder, she went to stay with her daughter in Gastonia, NC. After some time, it was decided she would move to an assisted living home in Gastonia and we have exchanged cards since then. She is a remarkable person, and has been such an inspiration to me! When my husband, Bill developed serious health problems, she would tell me that she'd look down and see our lights on and say a prayer for Bill.

At first our lot was all weeds and brush and red clay, except for a weeping willow on our side of the dividing line. The tree later died, but I have a snapshot and a memory of it. The picture is of our youngest daughter, Andrea, as a baby in her playpen—playing in the shade of the willow tree.

Mr. Cox bought his land for $275.00 in 1945. We, later, purchased this property from Mr. Cox for $1500.00 (1956). We were married in 1951 and rented a garage apartment from George

Holtzclaw in the 2nd block of Lancaster –in the direction of Ryan's Restaurant. The corporate offices of Ryan's across the street occupy a site once known as "The Greer Drive-In Theater."

I'll try to describe our walk-up apartment: the bathroom was at the end of the long entrance hall; to the right was the kitchen which covered the width of the first half of the apartment; the living room and bedroom covered the other half. A divider was behind the stove separating the living area from the kitchen. Across from the cooking area was a 'homemade' table with a linoleum top, usually covered with a tablecloth. The radio was at the end of the long, rectangular table. When Bill came to lunch, we ate and listened to "Ma Perkins," "Stella Dallas" or "Just Plain Bill."

Before we moved into the apartment, we ordered oil for the oil heater, which was in the kitchen. The "on" button had accidentally been turned on and the whole kitchen and living area were covered in oil, at least an inch thick!! Well, we were young and able to get it up—eventually, but it took some doing and a lot of rags and patience!!

I loved the apartment and the area—I think that is why we later bought the lot down the street. Our neighbors, the Anderson's were a sweet older couple. He called his wife, Miss Kitty. They had a garden, as did George and Alpha Holtzclaw, the owners. We often received vegetables from these gardens, thanks to our friendly neighbors.

We decided to get a couple of older kittens from the animal shelter and one immediately ran away. The other cat, a black cat, was afraid of everyone but me—if company came, she hid under our bed. She had kittens and her milk glands became infected. A trip to the vet was in order, but I had to get my mother to drive me—my husband refused (because of previous experience, traveling with cats). If you've ever been in a car with an animal (cat) who is not secure with strangers, much less in a closed area of a moving vehicle, you might have an inkling of what a trying experience this can be——especially when the cat gets out of the box and moves from the back to the front and vice-versa, all the while making "gosh-awful" meows!! Well, we made the 15-mile trip without an accident! Of course, we had the same trip on our return—but we at least knew what to do when we got home. The kittens had to be fed with "Di-dee Doll Bottles" because the mama cat couldn't nurse them; so we fed the little kittens. It required a great deal of persistence on our part and a lot of mewing and mauling on their part.

Bill worked for Smith and James, downtown men's clothiers in Greer, SC. He was a salesman and bookkeeper. In high school, I'd pass Smith and James as I walked to Frierson's where I worked on Saturdays. One day I went in Smith and James and Bill waited on me. He later called me for a date and the rest is history.

While we were living in the apartment on Lancaster, Bill developed viral pneumonia. Our doctor at the time was Dr. Marion L. Peeples. He advised Bill to stay in for two weeks and take prescribed medicine. I was not to sleep with him because the germ could be contagious—so, I made do on an army cot placed in the kitchen. I wonder now how I did that! It was not padded—just made of canvas and sagged a little in the center.

The old Piedmont –Northern Railway, now known as the Atlantic Coastline Railway, has tracks and railroad crossing not too far from Lancaster Avenue. In fact, the crossing is just below where the new library is—the Jean M. Smith Library on Aaron Tippin Drive. Lancaster Avenue ends where Aaron Tippin Drive begins.

As a young married woman, I remember being in bed and hearing the train whistle in the 'wee' hours of the morning. It would be a mournful sound. Even though it was dark, I'd still look out the window. You couldn't see the train or the crossing in the daytime from our apartment, much less at night—yet I looked out the window—I guess I just looked in the direction of the sound.

Chapter Thirty-One
The Harvey Children:
Beth, Chris and Andrea

After we settled into our Lancaster Ave. apartment, I was hired temporarily in the Victor Mill Office in Greer. I liked it very much but it was only temporary and I was transferred to the "Cloth Room" in the mill. The high windows and large rows of machines and brick walls and cement floors, made it stark and dreary—almost like a prison without any cells. Huge bolts of cloth were installed on a 'cloth' machine and a hand lever carried material down over a light. My job was to inspect the material for 'slubs' and imperfections. I could never make production—I guess I was too much of a perfectionist! Luckily, I became pregnant in this second year of our marriage and I happily handed in my resignation!

From our Lancaster Ave. apartment, we moved to my Mom and Dad's apartment on Church Street in Greer. Originally a garage, it was made into three rooms—Kitchen, Bedroom, Living area and a shower/bathroom. The difference in this garage apartment was that it was all ground level—no walk up. Even though I was pregnant (I don't remember how 'fragrant' I was) and wearing maternity clothes, I managed to paint our apartment—the smell of paint made Bill sick!

Our daughter, Lisa Beth was born that July and we were so happy—especially after the three-month cholic passed. How wonderful to be a mother! Beth was born three weeks early. I had no labor pains the day I went to the hospital (Spartanburg General) but my water had broken—and the 'book' said when that happened you needed to go to the hospital! Bill didn't want to go—he had a headache! Well, we did go and I was x-rayed and told to stay in bed not to get up. After being there all day, I was given a "Pit Drip" to bring on labor. That did the trick! It wasn't long before Beth was born. (I would later learn that the placenta had separated from the uterus and the afterbirth was coming first—a condition known as "Placenta Previa.")

Beth was so sweet. She weighed four pounds eight ounces. At five months I could put her in a little box, sit her on the kitchen table and talk to her while I did kitchen chores. It fit her so well that she was braced firmly and was happy sitting there. I wish we had a picture of her but I have it in my heart.

Except for the tin roof and summertime heat, we enjoyed living there. When Beth was two we began to realize our need for a home of our own. I went to work as a billing clerk at Bahan Textile Machinery Co. in Greenville, SC. I really didn't want to leave Beth; I enjoyed being with her so much. The first days at work, I'd think about her and wonder what she was doing...but an arrangement was worked out and Beth stayed with Bill's Aunt Gladys Foster. Sometimes her daughter, Dixie Foster took care of Beth. Dixie turned out to be an excellent baby-sitter who now (as Dixie Howard) has grandchildren of her own to baby sit. Beth was happy staying with Aunt Gladys.

My mother loaned me the money to buy a lot on Lancaster Ave. When we bought it, it was the last empty lot on the street. With my salary, I paid back the $1500 I had borrowed. Having the lot as collateral, we were able to get a bank loan from the Bank of Greer. Bill secured the loan from Mr. B. A. Bennett. He also asked his dad, Boyce Lee Harvey, Sr., if he would build our house—which he did, along with one other man, Bill Myers (the husband of Bill's Aunt Julie.) Being in construction work for most of his life, Mr. Harvey was experienced in building homes and carpentry. He was another family member who 'whistled while he worked.' I enjoyed his whistling and I appreciate the legacy he left us by building our house.

I worked approximately 2 ½ years, after which I stayed home with four year old Beth until her brother, Christopher Allen was born (1957)—another beautiful baby! Chris was born at Allen Bennett Hospital in Greer. Mama's maid, Millie McCray, was in the same hospital delivering her baby and my Dad was also there having gall bladder surgery. We all celebrated Thanksgiving of 1957 at Allen Bennett Hospital.

The next year our family doctor, Dr. Francis Sullivan, the doctor who delivered our son, Chris[and later our daughter Andrea] discovered I had a kidney stone and Dr. Kitt Smith performed surgery to remove the stone at Greenville General Hospital. It broke my heart to leave Chris and Beth. I cried as we pulled out of the driveway on our way to Greenville. Somehow I wanted them to be in their own bed at night and their routine to be the same even though I was in the hospital. Now that doesn't seem to be so important but then it meant a great deal to me. My Mother came to the hospital and used her nursing skills by staying with me for a couple of nights. She knew how to place pillows up against my back and side—how to make me more comfortable.

Granny came to see me in the hospital and after she left, she commented, "Toya is a rock." Coming from my Grandmother, Emmie, who suffered a broken pelvis and other trials of one sort or another, this compliment was appreciated. She was the one who had been a 'rock.' I hope I have inherited some of her strength!

Before going to the hospital, Chris was pulling up in his playpen. After two weeks in the hospital, he was taking steps when I came home. The next month we celebrated his first birthday, November 26th.

Our third child, Andrea Ellyn, came along three years after Chris was born, Aug. 29, 1960. How blessed we were! Another precious baby! She was probably the healthiest baby of all—but she was the longest in coming! I went to Allen Bennett Hospital the night before and stayed all night—finally she arrived at 1:00 P.M. the next day. God has blessed me with each child and given me such joy! How rewarding it is to be a Mother and how I love my children!! Of course, they're grown now and I have seven grandchildren to love!!

The young Harvey children: Beth, Chris and Andrea

Bill Harvey at desk in 'new Frierson's'

**The fountain in 'Old Frierson's;
Left to right: Ed Taylor, Jack Hammond (classmate of mine,
now desceased), Leon Hix and Louis Allen**

Chapter Thirty-two
PERSONALIZED TOUCH MADE FRIERSON'S DRUG STORE SPECIAL

Memories of a Former Soda Jerk
By Chris Harvey

Yes, I too was a soda jerk. I had the great opportunity of growing up in a drug store with a fountain. My grandfather, Dr. Louis Allen, purchased Frierson's Drug Store in 1957 and moved it from the original location on the corner of Randall and Trade (where Citizens Building & Loan is now located) to 209 Trade Street in 1959.

My father, Bill Harvey, (the man with the cigar) soon left his job a Smith & James to become manager of Frierson's. My mother, Toya, and my two sisters, Beth and Andrea also worked at Frierson's.

Several different families worked at Frierson's over the years, until it closed in 1977. My Aunt Betty and her daughters, also worked there. The Carpenter family with Sybil, Barry and Tim, and the Campbell family with Granny and Ruth also worked there. Former Greer Fire Chief Mack Bailey and his sister Kathy also were employed there.

Some of the more notable workers were Leon Hix, Frank Foster, Ed Taylor, just to mention a few. I could go on and on with names of people who worked at Frierson's.

The people at Frierson's always had a concern for the community. For example, I remember when Davenport Junior High School caught on fire, and my dad went to the drug store and made coffee all night for the fire fighters. Little did I know that a decade later, I would be working for the Greer Fire Department.

The fountain at Frierson's seemed to be a meeting place for the downtown area. The same crowd would come in every morning for coffee and lunch (we had great hot dogs). When school was out teenagers from Davenport and Greer High would come by for Cherry Cokes or a fresh dipped ice cream cone.

I personally spent many a day cleaning the grill or changing the oil in the deep fat fryer as part of my daily duties of cleaning the fountain area.

Frierson's had a Kay Nut Machine that myself and George Beason could not walk by without it grabbing us and making us get a handful of cashews to eat.

Besides being a soda jerk, I also was delivery boy. Some of my best memories are of making deliveries to customers. It seems like I went every week to Audrey and Mary Jordan's house. I also remember going to the Flatwood community and delivering medicine to the Bryant sisters. These darling ladies lived in a very old dilapidated house, but they were always thankful for what they had and seemed to cherish my visits. I always had to take a little extra time to listen to their stories or help them with a household chore that they could not do. The personalized touch of making home deliveries seemed to brighten many elderly citizens' days.

It was a sad day in January 1977 when my grandfather closed Frierson's because it was the last downtown drug store with a fountain operating at that time. Many children today do not even know what a fountain coke is. I guess you could say that Frierson's Drug Store was part of a dying breed of independent drug stores that provided the personalized touch to its customers.

Frierson's Drug Store played a big role in not only developing me personally, but many others, also.

(Editor's Note: Chris Harvey is now Fire Chief for the City of Greer, SC.)

This article was printed in The Greer Citizen, Wed. Apr 12, 2000.

Chapter Thirty-Three
My Interview with Toya Harvey

By: Meryl Phillips

This biography is about the life of Toya Allen Harvey. She took time out of her life to let me interview her for this class project. She was happy to help out with the interview. I hope that you have a wonderful time reading this.

[Meryl gives the names of Toya's parents; when they were married and where. She tells of the Depression; how Louis worked as a 'soda jerk' after graduating from the Medical College of Charleston with a degree in Pharmacy.] Meryl writes: It was a terrible time period. Money was so scarce.

Growing up in her family was very nice, sometimes. Toya and her family always used to go to her Granny's on Sundays to eat.

Toya lived in the country during World War II. She was about nine when she heard about the Pearl Harbor bombing over the radio. The war was a terrible and scary thing! The food had to be rationed and you had to have food coupons. You could buy only so many items at a time like eggs, butter, coffee, flour and gasoline.

[This paragraph tells of Toya's broken leg and the infection being so bad, she almost lost her leg.] There was a new drug and it cured the infection. Now she is up and running like nothing was ever wrong!

Some of the technology during her childhood was a lot like the things we have today. They had cars, trains, buses and airplanes. Many people didn't have enough money to have a car because they cost so much. So much that most people walked or took other transportation devices.

[The three children of Toya and Boyce (Bill) are named.] They had been married for two years when their first child, my Mother, Beth was born. Then their second child, Chris was born. Their last child, daughter, Andrea was born. They all had a happy life together.

Toya went to college after all the kids were born and in school themselves. She wanted to become a musician. So she went to college for six and a half years because she only went part time. She was raising three kids at the same time she was going to college. She became a musician. She did recitals and other musical things.

Toya has had a lot of memories throughout her lifetime. So she decided to share some of them with us today.

One memory that she remembers was when JFK died. She was picking up Beth and Chris from school when she heard about the murder of JFK. She heard it over the radio. She and another Mother were talking about it when Beth and Chris came out and said, "What is going on?" Then Toya told them.

Another memory that Toya remembers is when the whole family got in the car and went to Kentucky for a family vacation. They saw on the TV the first man on the moon. Toya says it was so thrilling—you wouldn't believe your eyes.

Also the memory of the spaceship explosion on January 26th, Toya was so upset. She and the family were in Greer and listening and watching TV when it happened.

The attack on the Trade Centers, on September 11, 2001, is another memory. It was so heartbreaking. She couldn't understand how someone could actually do something like that to our country. She watched it on TV but couldn't believe what she saw.

When I interviewed Toya Harvey I learned that she has done many things in her life. She has had great times with her family and she has seen terrible times in our country. She was happy to tell me about them.

My Grandmother, Toya Harvey, has had a life full of happy and sad times. She liked telling me about the things that have happened in her life.

Meryl Phillips, 6th grade, Greer Middle School
School Year: 2001-2002

Bill and Toya harvey when Bill was Lieutenant Governor of the Civitan District in their area - 1962-1963. Captions made are by their granddaughter, Meryl Phillips. Even though this was not our wedding picture, Meryl thought it was.

Grandma Toya & Meryl

Chapter Thirty-Four
Boyce L. Harvey, Jr.

Boyce, known to family and friends as Bill, graduated from Greer High School in 1947. He went to business school and became employed as bookkeeper and salesman for Smith and James, Greer, SC. After marriage he went to work for his father-in-law, Louis G. Allen as Manager of Frierson's Drug Store (See article from Greer Citizen by Chris Harvey about Frierson's Drug Store.) Bill successfully played a large role in closing out the business in the 1970's.

As a member of the National Guard since 1947, he began work for the Guard as Unit Administrator of the 178th FA Btn., Btry. B, at Inman, SC in the late 70's and worked until 1990. After falling and injuring his neck, he had surgery to remove a ruptured disc and spur. While hospitalized in Spartanburg Memorial Hospital, insulin treatment was started for diabetes' control. He retired at age 60.

After retirement, he and Toya were able to travel. A number of tours were taken—one out to California, New Mexico, Colorado (Pike's Peak), Texas (San Antonio, Riverwalk and the Alamo), Nevada (Las Vegas—wonderful stage show and meal), and Arizona. That was an exceptional trip! We saw the Grand Canyon and so much more.

Our son, Chris and his daughter, Amy took us to meet the tour bus before we left. Amy was just a little thing and she burst into tears at our leaving! I thought that was so sweet! She is still a tender- hearted person today.

Among other tours, was one to the Canadian Rockies, which was spectacular! We saw Lake Louise, Banf, Victoria (BC), Calgary, Vancouver, Seattle, Washington and Portland, Oregon. In Canada, we saw the Canadian mounted police and Bill had his picture taken with one of them. We took some shorter tours like the one to Wheeling, West Virginia and a Nashville tour, and a fall tour to Vermont. The one that stands out the most was the one I dearly loved, the tour to England! We took US Air and British Airways to London. From there we visited these cities: York, Oxford, Chester, Coventry, Bath, Stonehenge and Edinborough, Scotland. It was like stepping back in time. Chester was so quaint! All of it was impressive—cathedrals, Edinborough Castle, Salisbury, thatched-roof houses, old architecture! Wish we could go back!!

Bill developed Cushing's disease and because of neglect of lab work analysis, his thyroid had to be removed. The radioactive capsule didn't take and it had to be done again a year later. Once he recovered from this, he had surgery to remove 2/3 of his Pituitary Gland—there were numerous little tumors because of Cushing's disease. Miraculously he recovered and manages fairly well. He has degenerative disc disease in the spine and this causes severe back pain. God has blessed him and made it possible to function in spite of angioplasty in 1998.

Bill is a person of quick wit, having inherited his mother's Irish sense of humor! When he was getting acupuncture treatments for back pain, he always said something to the receptionist to make her laugh. One day, the receptionist saw me before she saw Bill, and she asked, "Is Stinky Here?" It is so nice to meet friendly faces with time to smile and joke with Bill. Thank goodness for Bill's sense of humor and his toughness in enduring the illnesses he has been through.

Bill Harvey, Sr., Lillian Harvey and Billy Harvey

161

Chapter Thirty-five
Lillian, Betty and Jean
The Harveys and Victor Baptist Church
Tribute to Pastor Boles by Amy Harvey

Bill's Mother, Lillian Lister Harvey, a good cook, was always inviting us to eat with her. A generous person, she gave us two pecan trees, two maple trees and four camellia bushes to put out around our house. In addition to these, she gave us a number of azaleas to set out. When the children were small, she often bought clothes for them.

Bill, the middle child, had an older sister, Betty Lou and a younger sister, Peggy Jean. Jean and I were in the same grade and finished Greer High School together. She was also one of my bridesmaids when we married. Betty married Harold Waters and when the baby of the family, Susan was very young—maybe four or so, Harold died. This left Betty, not only with four children: Cynthia, Tony, Cathy and Susan to rear but also The Fork Restaurant to manage! And manage she did for many years. Later she kept Mrs. Harvey (Lillian) in her home—in a comatose state for about two years. Betty married again to Bill Vaden and his Mother lived with them until she died. Now Betty has recovered from open-heart surgery and she and Bill have a dog to keep them company. Bill Vaden died October, 2005.

Jean married Landrum Smith and they had a son, Brian Smith. Landrum died in May of 2002. I had written in my journal that Jean had adjusted and was living alone. Unfortunately she had to start taking insulin shots and she told me she didn't know how to do it but someone she knew would 'walk her through' the process over the phone. Something happened—we believe she gave herself too much insulin—and she was found in a coma (February 3, 2003.) She never regained consciousness. Such a sad situation!

I have not attempted to do research on the Harvey-Lister ancestors, except the family trees that are located in this book. Maybe there will be a family member who will take this on as a project.

There is a section in Greer, SC, known as "Harvey Road." This area was owned and farmed by Bill's grandfather, John Harvey. The "old home place" across from the American Legion Ball Park, was torn down and Bill's Aunt Kathleen, her husband 'Ram' Smith, along with Bill's Uncle, Jim Harvey built a brick home on the site. On this site will be the 'new' Victor Baptist Church. Victor Baptist has bought the property and plans are being made for the new church to be built. This is the church where Bill, Betty and Jean were members at one time. Today, my son, Chris and his wife, Donna— along with Justin and Amy are members there. One of the highlights of the Christmas season was to visit Victor Baptist for their Candlelight Service. Chris, Donna and Amy took me with them. Another highlight of Christmas (2003) was going with Beth and David to our church, The Lutheran Church of Our Saviour for the Candlelight Service on Christmas Eve. Of course, our family got together on Christmas Eve day for another great Christmas celebration. Our Grandson, Justin Harvey, a fireman with Piedmont Park Fire Department was on duty Christmas Eve and also on Thanksgiving. We missed having him with us but he called and everyone spoke with him on the phone. Later, daughter Andrea and her husband Joe and family went by the Fire Department to see him. Justin dropped by a few days later to see us. Reader, I'm sure you can see how much family means to us and to me!! As an 'only' child, it is so rewarding to have the love and support of all the family!

My Granddaughter, Amy Harvey, has written an essay concerning a former pastor of Victor Baptist church:

The Most Influential Person in My Life

I have been most fortunate to be surrounded by so many positive role models. I admire my mother's strength, my father's courage and my brother's perseverance. These three people have been an inspiration in my life. However, someone else has greatly influenced me into the person I am today. The most influential person in my life has been my former preacher, Edgar Boles, or as I call him, "Pastor Boles."

Pastor Boles came into my life when I was just entering middle school. I was eleven and I did not care much about church. I went to church to see my friends and socialize. I was a Christian but I never studied my Bible or listened to the boring sermons. I was much too busy passing notes to my friends. However, everything changed when Pastor Boles began preaching. I started to realize the meaning of those complicated Scriptures. I actually enjoyed singing those dull hymns. Preaching became a time of learning about Jesus and His awesome gift! Of course, our former minister preached the same message, but somehow Pastor Boles opened my eyes, my ears and most of all, my heart.

Pastor Boles left our church on Christmas Eve. I was sixteen and heartbroken. I never realized what Pastor Boles meant to me until he left. I still remember saying goodbye and how I tried so hard not to cry. I knew it would not be the last time I saw him, but it felt like a phase of my life had ended. Whether he realized it or not, Pastor Boles helped me through some difficult years of my life. Whenever I needed him, Pastor Boles was there. He helped not only me, but also my family through some rough times.

I will always have the highest regard for Pastor Boles. I am so grateful that God brought him into my life. His kindness will always stay with me. The lessons that he taught me have changed me into a better person. I can only hope that one day I will be as influential as my preacher was for me.

Written November 1, 2003

164

Note: Amy Harvey was the editor of the 2004 Yearbook for Greer High School and was was among those chosen to be in the Senior Gallery of the Yearbook. Amy has always been a good student— she ranked fifth in her class. Now she is a sophomore student at Winthrop University ! { September 8, 2005.}

Amy harvey in Paris, France

Amy Harvey on Santa's lap and Pastor Boles in the doorway

Chapter Thirty-Six
Thanks Be to God

"Bless O Lord this food to our use and us to thy loving service,
Make us ever mindful of and responsive to the needs of others."

My son, Christopher Harvey was taught this blessing by his
elementary school teacher, a Mrs. Williams. She took a special
interest in Chris and even invited him to go fishing with her and
her husband. How kind and perceptive she was. I'm sure Chris
appreciated her interest, especially when his mother was so busy
with college courses and teaching piano on the side—plus practicing piano two hours every day (a minimum requirement of piano
majors.) While I practiced, Bill took Beth, Chris and Andrea to
ride to visit relatives or sometimes to antique auctions. At the
time, Bill had quite an interest in auctions—In fact, I never knew
what he'd come home with. One time he didn't tell me what he
bought the night before, he just told me to look out on the front
porch! Well, imagine my exasperation when I looked out and saw
an old pump organ centered on the porch! Usually Bill didn't pay
attention to what I said, but he listened when I said it had to go!!
At that time we couldn't afford the organ and he was finally per-
suaded to sell it. He made up for this extravagance later, when He
bought me a refinished baby grand piano for a Mother's Day present. This was while I was still in college, just before I transferred
to Bob Jones University.

The phrase, "make us ever mindful of and responsive to the
needs of others," is descriptive of the kind of person Chris is—ever
mindful of and responsive to the needs of others. As Fire Chief
here in Greer, this phrase is certainly meaningful to him and all the
other firefighters, as well.

One year, Bill was sick on my birthday and didn't go to
work. Now when Bill was sick, the world around him just stopped
until he felt better. Nothing would have stirred him to even say

"Happy Birthday" until he rested a day or so. The children must have thought I needed cheering up because as I was washing the dishes and looking out the kitchen window, I saw Chris and Andrea Painting "Happy Birthday, Toya" on their old barn-red tree house. They painted it in white and made the letters large enough that it could easily be seen 40 feet away! I'm sure it was Chris's idea, but Andrea, and the Latimer children (our neighbors) helped. This greeting was never painted over (I cherished it). The tree house just had some sides and a roof that Bill had built for the children to play in. It was built over a shed where our lawnmower was kept and where dear "Sparky", our Dalmatian stayed. What a good dog Sparky was! Originally he was Chris's dog but after Chris married, Sparky stayed with us. Such a faithful companion he was to all of us. Sparky would even let me give him a bath. It wasn't easy but we were in the backyard, and even though he'd back away and run from me, he'd still come back and somehow we'd get through. He soon had company, — a stray kitten began staying under the back steps and eventually became tame enough to come out and eat. After awhile, Sparky and "Little Bit" the new kitten, became buddies. They'd loll in the sun on our picnic table. For some reason, Little Bit liked to chew on Sparky's ear and Sparky never seemed to mind. He liked Little Bit and they were good companions. Something happened to Little Bit; he just disappeared and Sparky was left alone to dig up holes in the yard as he looked for chipmunks. I could never plant flowers because Sparky would dig them up. As Sparky aged he developed arthritis; his hind legs dragged as he tried to walk. He also became blind and he couldn't see where he was going— so it was time for him to "go to sleep." He was the best dog we ever had!!

We had many cats and kittens as the children were growing up. My piano students told me their friends wanted to know, "Did they take lessons from the 'cat lady?'" One of our neighbors died, and left a 'calico' cat. She had previously asked if someone would take her cat——well, Guess who did? "Mama Kitty" was always having kittens! The children brought the cats into our house now and then but they didn't stay in the house—they were not actually house pets; however one litter of kittens was born under Andrea's bed (in Beth and Andrea's room.) Andrea especially liked cats as did Beth, but Andrea was the one who truly enjoyed playing with them. She had picnics with one cat, a beautiful male tabby with orange/gold fur. Andrea would sit across from the cat while he ate out of a tuna can and she ate something like a cookie, or sandwich, in a little dish. She still loves cats, and today in her home she, Joe and all their children enjoy their two cats, Smoky and Nasty!

Beth enjoyed playing with her 'Barbie doll' at the fence with Sylvia Duncan. They'd bring their 'Barbie's out to the fence in our back yard. Beth's Barbie had received some outfits for Christmas that I made; I remember a dress, a raincoat, a party dress (some of the items.) Occasionally, I made dresses for Beth and Andrea—although I was not naturally gifted in the sewing department—as Beth used to say when complimented on her new dress, "Mama went right by the Pattern!" Not only did Beth and Sylvia play at the fence, Chris and Sylvia's brother, Heyward played with their 'dump-trucks' there. How I enjoyed watching them from the kitchen window! I always said I couldn't imagine living anywhere else; I wanted to be able to see the children and I can still look out and remember them climbing up the ladder into the tree house.

Andrea and her friend, Cece McCormick were usually on the front porch with the kittens and paper dolls, games and Barbie dolls. Sometimes they had an argument and Cece went home, but not before Andrea tried to bribe her to stay—offering her some bread and water! If I didn't have anything like cookies to eat, Andrea wasn't supposed to offer food unless it was all right with me. After pleading with Cece to come in, Cece told her, "No thank you, I don't want any bread and water!"

Sparkey Adds His "Merry Christmas"

"Merry Christmas everyone." Sparkey a Dalmation owned by Greer City Fireman Chris Harvey, appeared to be saying to those along the trade route Wednesday during Greer's Christmas Parade. Sparkey, was driven in a fire truck by Harvey and with the exception of Santa, delighted children the most.

Saturday February 22, 2003: Justin Harvey graduated from the Fire Academy Columbia, SC. I attended the ceremony with his father, mother and sister—Chris, Donna and Amy Harvey. Now Justin is a fireman with Wade Hampton Fire Department, Greenville, SC.

**Our son, Chris Harvey and his family:
Chris, Donna, Justin and Amy**

Chapter Thirty-Seven
Moving Along in the Seventies

The Vietnam War ended with a cease-fire in 1973. Lack of support for the war and terrible fighting conditions in Vietnam caused some of our fighting men to turn to drugs. The "70's" saw increased drug trade, narcotic dealers and drug addicts—in the United States this was especially seen in the "Haight-Ashbury District" of San Francisco.

The 'love-child' hair garlands and flowing print dresses reflected the look and attitude of the 'flower'children—the "make love not war" expressions of many young people. Mini-skirts and thigh-high boots were also popular and were seen on television as well as in public. Two TV shows that depict the ambience of the 70's were "Sonny and Cher" and "Laugh-In."

Fortunately, life went on in spite of the war and drug problems. The musical influence was innovative—combinations of new sounds, talented arrangements and musical groups. The legacy of these groups is still heard and enjoyed today: The Beatles, the Beach Boys, the Bee Gee's, the Carpenter's and Simon and Garfunkle—and many more! I can't name them all but I can say the music was singable and it was a pleasure to turn on the radio or the TV and to hear the music.

Shopping recently, at a grocery outlet I had the experience of wanting to sing along as the 'piped-in' music of the 60's and 70's was played. Not only I, but a lady in the 'cookie' aisle was singing with the music and as I waited in the check-out line, a gentleman and his wife were humming and singing, also! It seemed to brighten everyone's day! I can't say that for the music you hear in many shops and restaurants. It should be background music, but it's "in your face" or "kill your ears"—a type I can't call music, just sound repeated over and over without any melody or redeeming qualities. What happened to good music?

I was finishing my last college courses in the fall and winter of 1972 at Bob Jones University in Greenville, SC. The outstanding music department; excellent instruction from piano teacher, Lawrence Morton; and gifted teaching from music theory teacher, Dr. Frank Garlock were great challenges! Dr. Garlock used to say: "How full do you want your cup?"

I gave my Senior Recital April 10, 1970 at age thirty-seven. My music courses were completed but I had other courses to complete: English 309, Renaissance Literature [1485-1660] and History 320, the Middle Ages. The reguirements for Eng 309 included a major paper, approximately 12 typewritten pages; the topic approved by instructor, Dr. Horner. Since I was writing a paper for Mr. McGuire in Hi 320, the Middle Ages, I decided to utilize some of my research on my paper, The Miracle Plays of the Middle Ages. For my Eng 309 paper I chose the topic, Elizabethan Drama and the Dramatic Forms that Preceded It. My purpose: to show the development of drama from the early church presentations to Miracle Plays in the church; followed by plays in and outside the church; to secular presentations for the people and by the people (not the clergy); to presentations at court.

Stories in Scripture were enacted and presented in church as a means of teaching Scripture to people who could not read. Miracle Plays made use of Biblical stories. The Morality Plays were attempts at teaching morals based on Scripture. People began to act out stories for their own enjoyment—sometimes humorous and sometimes sad. The famous writers Shakespeare and Marlowe wrote historical plays and 'comedies.' Shakespeare, known for his chronicle plays and comedies, and tragedies, spoke the language of the common man. The popularity of his plays was shown by crowds attending the production of his plays at the Globe Theater in London.

Both papers, The Miracle Plays of the Middle Ages and Elizabethan Drama and the Dramatic forms that Preceded It were dated December 4, 1972—one for History and one for English. English was my minor and the A+ from Dr. Horner was well received as was the comment, "A thorough Piece of Work." From Mr. McGuire, I received an A-.

The relationship of history and literature are such that you are learning history when you study literature and learning literature when studying history! History must have literature to tell the story, while literature must have history to present the facts!

My daughter, Beth was a freshman at Winthrop College in 1972 (Rock Hill, SC) My son Chris was fifteen and daughter Andrea was twelve and I was thirty-nine. One was in college, one in high school and one in middle school. Beth blossomed in college. Always serious, she made new friends, did new things and (in spite of course-work) had fun!

Chris had his own grass-cutting service. With his Dad's help and a trailer to haul the riding lawnmower, he had a number of customers. He even cut grass in Greenville for an apartment complex. He became interested in 'drag-racing' and was involved in it on week-ends. Bill signed a note for Chris to get his own car when he was fifteen.

Andrea often went with Bill and me (as did Chris) to visit Beth at Winthrop. One time, Andrea and I were coming back from Rock Hill after dark and a heavy rain forced us off the road. From the driver's side I didn't see that we were about to go over an embankment. Andrea warned me and I tried to pull back but the front right wheel wouldn't budge. I remember Andrea getting out and telling me the wheel was at the edge. The rain was pouring and Andrea was so upset; she was crying, actually seeing the danger we were in! After some time, a pick-up truck pulled up with three young men. They hopped out to see what the situation was and saw I couldn't back up [and I sure couldn't go forward or we'd have gone over that bank.] The men determined that each one would sit on one of the fenders and the traction from their weight might help—-They were right! That made all the difference—we were able to back up!! We were ever so grateful to the 'three angels sitting on the fenders!'

I began college study at North Greenville College when Andrea was in the 1st grade and Chris was in 3rd grade at Tryon St. Elementary and Beth was in Davenport Junior High. Those schools have been replaced. Davenport burned down and Tryon St., demolished. I was a part-time student taking only morning classes—that way I could still pick up the children at school. Upon completing two years at North Greenville, I transferred to Bob Jones University. Luckily all my course-work transferred to BJU and I didn't lose any credits.

Once Beth graduated from Winthrop College [now Winthrop University] she started teaching in McCall, SC and Cheraw, SC. When a position opened at Tryon St. in Greer, she returned home. Later she took a position at East Greer Elementary and now teaches at Chandler Creek Elementary in Greer. [Correction, she is now teaching kindergarten (as of Sept. 2005, Lutheran Church of Our Saviour Day School.]

Chris graduated from High School in 1976 and Andrea in 1978. Andrea started to Winthrop, the fall of 1978. One day as I was getting ready to teach piano [as I did in my home] a knock came at the door and I opened it thinking it was one of my students but to my surprise, there stood Andrea! "Am I in time for my piano lesson?" she asked—one of many 'silver' moments. After one semester at Winthrop, Andrea became distracted by Joe O'Shields and they were married in June of 1978 at Redeemer Lutheran Church, Greer, SC. Andrea worked for a year or two before Ashley O'Shields was born (1981.) The same year Chris married Donna Arms. Allison O'Shields was born 1982 and Justin Harvey [Chris and Donna's son] was born 1983. Brandon O'Shields was born 1984 1985, Amy Harvey [Chris and Donna's daughter] was born 1986 and Toya O'Shields was born 1987.

174

Beth married David Phillips in 1985 and Meryl Phillips was born 1990. Beth and David had their wedding at Redeemer Lutheran Church in Greer. Chris and Donna were married at Victor Baptist in Greer. Chris was a fireman working under Chief Mack Bailey.

When Andrea's children were old enough, she enrolled in a Nursing program at Greenville Technical College. After completing her work, she transferred to Clemson College where she earned her degree, Bachelor of Science in Nursing. Her age was 38. Just one year's difference that when I did, [age 39 at BJU.]

Thanksgiving at Andrea's
From left to right: Beth Phillips, David Phillips, Donna
Harvey, Chris Harvey, Joe O'Shields and Andrea O'Sheilds

Chapter Thirty-Eight
I Know Why the Grass Is Green

The year 1998, Andrea O'Shields graduated from Clemson. Her daughter Allison, age 16 had three essays published in Wren High School Magazine. Here is one of them.

<u>I Know Why the Grass Is Green</u>

I really believe and I know for a fact that the grass is green. Now I know what you're thinking, this chick is weird, but let me explain myself. I thought about what I absolutely, without a doubt believed in, and the only thing I could think of was that the grass was green. If somebody came up to me and said that the grass was green, I would say, "You know what, you're absolutely right." If someone came up to me and said that abortion was right or wrong, I wouldn't know what to believe. Personally, I don't have beliefs on anything because I don't know what to say or think about that particular topic.

I question everything, even my own faith, and because of this, I can't come to a conclusion about anything. This is very frustrating for me, and I think that it's really sad, but there's nothing I can do about it. Whenever I am involved in an argument about topics that affect teens or anything in general, I just throw out information on that particular subject. Therefore, people say I constantly contradict myself.

Overall, the point I'm trying to make is that I know the grass is green and it always will be. I have no reason to question that, but if someone told me that abortion or being gay was right or wrong, I would just have to nod my head and keep going because I JUST DON'T KNOW WHAT TO BELIEVE.

Allison O'Shields, 11th Grade
Wren High School, Piedmont, SC

I love Allison's honesty as she shares with the reader her doubts about her beliefs. Today she has definite beliefs, especially her belief in God. Her statement: "If I've learned nothing else, I've learned that God will supply every need." This statement is found in the Chapter Forty - Brazil 2001 Journal.

Allison O'Shields

Wedding Party: Ashley O'Shields, Bill Harvey, Toya Harvey, Allison Cawley, Brian Cawley, Andrea O'Shields, Joe O'Shields, Toya O'Shields and Brandon O'Shields

Chapter Thirty-Nine
NATIONAL FORESTRY ALERT
EASLEY, SC AREA

This is an Email sent by my son, Chris Harvey to his sister, Andrea O'Shields on her birthday, August 29, 2000.

NATIONAL FORESTRY ALERT EASLEY, SC AREA

The US Forestry Service has issued a ban on burning for the Easley, SC area. All fire departments in the upstate have been requested to be on 24-hour standby on August 29.

The forestry service has learned that August 29, 2000 is your 40th birthday and we are concerned that if you have a birthday cake with candles, we possibly will have the same conflagration that is going on out west. Simply put, if you light your birthday candles, there will not be enough firefighters in the United States to put out the fire it will cause. People like you don't need to be close to fire anyhow--you risk catching your clothes on fire and we don't think you can still STOP, DROP, and ROLL. It's more like--"I've fallen and I can't get up!" Plus at your age you just can't move fast in support hose and a walker! We also have alerted your co-workers at St. Francis Hospital to prevent you from lighting any birthday candles and to remind you about the little things--like showing up for work with your teeth in, and remembering to pull up your pants after relieving yourself in what you thought was the bathroom. Security has also been alerted to look for you every day and help you find your way to the emergency room to work. In closing, you will be receiving a bill for all the manpower that is on standby for your birthday. Just remember some men feel that older women are sexy; I think it's one out of every ten billion! Happy Birthday and remember for the safety of all the tri-state area. please don't light any candles for your birthday!

The US Forestry Service

Ashley O'Shields holding baby

Andrea O'Shields and ~~Rick Banks~~ working in tent

Correction

Dr. Greg Langley

Chapter Forty
Missionary Bios, Brazil 2000

The O'Shields Family

The entire O'Shields family—Joe, Andrea, Ashley, Allison, Brandon and Toya—is going to Brazil. The O'Shields' live in Easley, SC. Joe works with Henderson Plumbing Services where he installs and repairs plumbing systems. Andrea works as a registered nurse in the ER at St. Francis Health Systems. The O'Shields have been married 20-years, they've lived in Easley 19 years and have been members of First Baptist Church of Easley 18 years. Joe was born in Durham, NC. Andrea was born in Greer. Joe is a member of the Property and Grounds Committee. Andrea is a member of the Sanctuary Choir and the Master's Blend Singers. Joe's hobbies are working on cars, working in the yard and sports. Andrea's hobbies are reading, attending children's soccer games, music and collecting antiques.

It took the O'Shields family one to two months to decide to be a part of the Brazil Mission Trip. Joe will work on the Construction Team and Andrea will serve on the Medical Team. Joe hopes to grow in his relationship with God, to help others grow, also to help build a place for the Brazilian people to worship. Andrea hopes to make an impact on the Brazilians but she expects an even greater impact on her family by the Brazilians.

Emails, June 2000

Sunday, June 18th
[From Toya to Andrea] Hello there! I see you made it! I'm checking your web site every day. Still saying those prayers! We watched you take off after you waited 30 minutes. Hope everybody made the trip okay and had no trouble at customs. It's pretty hot

still but we have had some rain, probably not enough, tho'. Happy Father's Day to you, Joe and to all the fathers! Bill fell during the night; he got off balance getting out of bed and split his lip on the chest of drawers but I think it will be okay. I didn't get to church because we were up at 2:00 a.m., 3:00 a.m., and 5:00 a.m. His lip wouldn't stop bleeding. After changing pillowcases and undershirts and applying ice and bandages, it seems to be checked.

I guess you all are familiar with your sleeping patterns being changed aren't you? I wonder how you managed with the changeover to the time there. I'm sure everybody was tired and anxious to get to a place of rest—such as a bed! God bless you and keep you in his care.
> Love you,
> Mom

Sunday June 18th
[From Andrea to Toya and Bill] Hey Daddy and Mama, Happy father's day Daddy. We finally got here yesterday around 3:00. We went right through Customs without being checked. God is truly watching over us. A piece of our luggage got left in Sao Paulo we're supposed to get it today. Luckily we had a change of clothes in our carry-on bags, except I forgot to put some underwear for Joe in the carry-on. The sink comes in handy for washing clothes. We're going to Bolivia today for rest and relaxation. I love you and will talk to you later.

> Deus te ama,
> Andrea, Joe, Allison, Brandon, and Toya

Wednesday, June 21st
[From Andrea to Toya] Hey Daddy and Mama,
I'm writing to you on my break. I'm sitting in a tent on a dirt floor in the land settlement where we are working. The people live in shacks without water or electricity and walk around barefoot or

wear flip-flops. It is a little warmer here today. It has been cold until now. Our luggage arrived on Sunday intact. We are treating a lot of people. We have seen around 400 patients. I am triaging patients in the morning and helping a dentist in the afternoon. The people are very friendly and appreciative of our efforts. Everyone is doing fine. God is truly blessing our family. Hope you are doing fine. I will try and write to you later. Tell Chris that Carl King pastored at Victor Baptist Church in the 80's and said he remembers Chris. I love you.

Deus te ama,
Andrea

Thursday June 22nd
[From Toya to Andrea] Andrea,
It was good to hear from you. We've gotten both of you letters. I called Vivian [Joe's Mother, Vivian O'Shields] after we got the first one to let her know you and Joe were okay. I'm sure there are many lessons you're learning from this experience! I enjoy reading the updates that are on "Brazil 2000" everyday. I've saved some of the pictures and have them in 'my documents.' You all are doing a wonderful work! I know God is pleased! Just a "cup of water in Jesus' name" and "you have done it unto Him!" How inspiring, all that you are doing. I know it must be exhausting, seeing so many patients and maybe feeling limited as to how much can be done in just two weeks, but God will bless your efforts and as you said, you will all be changed! God bless you all and keep you in His care. We had a good visit to Gatlinburg. Our friend, Nancy (Riskevics) went with us. We saw two shows, Southern Nights and The Blackwood Bros. Quartet. Both shows were good, wholesome and had a spiritual message. The Southern Nights show ended with the hymn, How Great Thou Art. Most of the Blackwood show had religious quartet numbers but they also did songs that were popular through the 50's to the present. Ron Blackwood spoke about the moral decline in America today and how we all need to get on our knees to honor Christ! He spoke about the messages the young

people are getting from our society—he described it as 'garbage in and garbage out.' May the young people on this trip to Brazil get the 'real message of honoring Christ and serving Him.' I pray that our Lord will protect all of you and all of us from evil. Will write more later.

Love,
Mama

Saturday, June 24th
[From Andrea to Toya] Hey Daddy and Mama,
How are you doing? We are working very hard, but the work is rewarding. Joe, Brandon, and Toya went fishing early this a.m. but didn't catch anything. Ashley, Allison, and I went on a boat trip on the Paraguay River today. It was fun. We have seen over 1000 patients this week. The weather has become very hot. Everyone is doing fine. Tell everyone hello. We love you. Keep checking the web site. Happy Anniversary early.

Love,
Andrea

Sunday, June 25th
[From Toya to Andrea, Joe, Ashley, Allison, Brandon and Toya O'Shields]
Hey there! Hope you all have had some rest on your break. Thanks Andrea for the E-mail and remembering our anniversary. The pictures are really good. I've put most of them in my "photo organizer" under "Printmaster." Went to church and sat by my friend, Sadie Dominick. Told her about you and the trip to Brazil. She said she lived in Brazil in Rio for 3-years and her daughter was 6-years old at the time. She said she learned Portuguese well—the daughter, that is. Sadie said she could only speak enough to get by. When you get back, maybe you could meet her and talk over Brazil. She commented about how often it rained and most of the children

didn't have shoes. Chris said he remembered Carl King. He has tuned in to the web address for Brazil 2000 and downloaded some of the pictures. Bill says to say hello to you. I guess our temperature and the temperature there in Brazil is almost the same—hot!! I think it is wonderful how God is using all of you; showing His love, healing in His name, and spreading the Gospel. I pray for you all and also the people you're ministering to. God bless all of you and keep you in His care.

Love you so much!
Mom, Grandmama, and Friend

Andrea O'Shields

Joe O'Shields

185

Chapter Forty-One
Poetry of Toya O'Shields

My Fear

I run and run away from my fear
Running fast
Not letting it get near
Running from my past

Tears pour
Heart is in two
Happiness is no more
Nothing is true

Run and run
Down, down
Can't see the sun
Only my frown

Through all the briers
My skin tears
Because of the liar
Because of the scares

Picking up my pace
Trying not to fall
Tears run down my face
No one hears my call

The road is slippery now
Am I going to fall?
Stay up? But how?
My fears getting big and making me small

TOYA ALLEN HARVEY

I'm getting very weak
The water is getting deep
Strength, I seek
That's what I need to keep

I start to swim
And I turn around
Everything is so dim
But I hear the loud sound

My heart is pounding
I'm getting cold
The puddle is rounding
I can't keep my hold

Screaming, I say
Give me strength!!!
This isn't my day
The puddle is longer in length

I hear the thunder
Of my fear
I start to wonder
How it's getting so near

The thought is in my head
I start to ponder
Am I almost dead
Then I start to wander

I go another way
But it's still there
It won't go away
It has no care

Boom, Bang!
Splash, Splash
My ears rang
As the water splashed

I am so sad
I am still crying
How can it be so bad
Honest, I'm trying

Then, my fear caught up with me
And swallowed me whole
Now, I am never to be
Because I've lost my soul.

**Toya O'Shields teaching a Bible lesson with the help of a
Brazilian interpreter**

Chapter Forty-Two
Brazil 2001 Journal

On Sunday, June 24th, a Commissioning Service was held at Easley First Baptist for the Brazil Volunteers. Donations of time, talent and preparation took place before the Second Missionary Trip to Brazil became a reality.

From Ramona Lewis's exceptional Journal accounts of the volunteers' activities in Corumba, Brazil, I have selected and condensed certain sections that relate to the O'Shields' family:

We are here! All 51 of us. We had a long tiring 36 hours of travel but our God was with us every minute, intervening with short waiting lines in some places and patience when that was not the case. However, we made it through customs with no problems and with all our supplies. A few of our men were diverted for luggage search, and one of them was Brandon O'Shields. Since all six of the O'Shields family are with our group, their mountain of luggage was distributed among the family members and 16 year-old Brandon happened to have some of nurse Mom's luggage on his cart. The custom officials wanted to open the locked pieces that only Andrea had the key for, but Brandon kept a cool head, explained the situation to the official, went to get his mom; they okayed everything and we were on our way. I think Joe and Andrea were more concerned about them confiscating Brandon than any of the medical supplies she was carrying.

[The first working day]
This morning at six o'clock, we hit the floor running. At 7:00 the buses pulled out with the medical team and the construction team on board, ready and anxious to begin the work that God has sent them here to do. The children's ministry team followed as soon as the buses could make a second run. For all but 22 of the volunteers, this is a first-time experience. Some are in for an emotional shock when they visit the land settlement for the first time. Some are

returning to a people they have already learned to love and they are experiencing "emotional overload." For all, this day will be one we will never forget. TO GOD BE THE GLORY.

[12 July]
I spent the morning and part of the afternoon with the children's ministry team as they conducted Bible School at the settlement. We are averaging around two hundred children daily now. The most favorite thing in the whole world to the children is singing. They just love to sing, and of course, the livelier, the better. Their favorite song is, "Celebrate Jesus, Celebrate" with hand motions. It's also the favorite of the workers because that's one they can sing in Portuguese!

I wish you could see how the children swarm over Ashley O'Shields and Sarah Dodson. These two young ladies sure have impressed me with their spiritual maturity.

After a delicious supper here at the hotel, we all boarded buses again and went across town to New Corumba Baptist Church. This church is about two years old. The building was built by a Mission Team from Mississippi. A song festival had been planned by them and The First Baptist Church for our benefit. We were treated to a rendition of "Holy Ground" sung by the King Family. Also, our own Ashley O'Shields and Lorie King sang a duet.

The Pantavida, a medical missionary boat left Tuesday {July 10} with a group of our missionaries to travel up the Paraguay to give medical treatment and the Gospel to people living on the vast networks of rivers in Brazil.

[This Email from Andrea speaks of daughter, Allison as one of the 27 people on the Pantivida] Hey, Mama and Daddy, I am finally getting to send you an email. I have been getting your mail,but I haven't been able to send out mail because of a server problem. Everybody is doing fine. Allison left yesterday on the boat and will be gone until next Wednesday. She and two other people will be doing children's activities at several isolated ranches while medical

services are rendered. The boat has bunk beds in very small quarters, but there is air condition. I wanted Allison to stay on land, but she really wanted to go. Kelle my nurse friend and another woman from my church told me they would take care of her. I know she will be fine and is in God's hands. Continue to pray for us. God is doing marvelous things here. Thank you for visiting the cats and checking on the garden. Tell everyone we said hello. Hope you and Daddy are well. I love you and will try to write again.
Love,
Andrea

p.s. Keep the mail coming.

[19 July: a condensed portion of Ramona Lewis's account of The Return of the Boat People]
The agenda for the boat people went something like this: two days traveling on the river to get to the first town, Puerto Bahianegra, (Black Bay) Paraguay. Stayed there two days, then down river for a 45 minute ride to a little Indian village called Puerto Diana where they stayed two more days. Then two days travel back up the river to Corumba. There were 27 people on a 65 ft. boat with 6 women living in a 7 x 7 room for eight days. No one remembered hearing a complaint or unkind word. Sacrifice wasn't an issue, service was. Allison O'Shields said that if she learned nothing else, she learned that God will supply every need. [continuing] In Bahianegra, were two missionary couples living there. This little town is so remote that it takes two days travel on the river by boat to get to the nearest Spanish – speaking people. There is no access to the town by land, no roads. And these people don't speak Portuguese or Spanish. They have their own native language, therefore only the missionary couples could interpret for our group. Patty Lawton was on board to work with the children as was Allison. O'Shields. They couldn't communicate through language so they played games with them and sang songs with them and loved them but they couldn't tell about Jesus. Patty left her puppet with the missionary couple's six year old son on the condition that he would tell the Indian children a story about how God can change people as he could change the puppet from a 'tadpole on the outside to a frog on the inside.'

191

[18 July]
Did you see the pictures of the loooong lines of people waiting? When the construction crew arrived at 6:30 this morning, there were an estimated 250 people and some had come as early as 4:30 a.m. The lines continued to grow and our people continued to minister and try to meet the needs of hurting people.

[20 July]
The whole construction project is remarkable! It was hard to believe that all that needed to be done could be done in nine days—but it was done! Now a five bedroom dorm will sleep 26 people comfortably in air conditioned rooms. There is a new kitchen and parlor. Out back is a bathhouse with eight showers and eight toilets and six sinks. This facility will be used as a retreat center for Baptists from all over the state of Mato Grosso do Sol, as well as housing for mission groups. A high school student, Brandon O'Shields was finishing stucco walls. Joe O'Shields (a Master Plumber) repaired existing pipes and installed new ones.

[The 2nd week, workers moved to another area, a "sub-division' the site of the Pantanal Project Center]
At the entrance of the sub-division stands a concrete statue of Jesus that is about 12 to 15 feet high. The whole city, the whole area knows that we are here and what we are doing. The local TV station sent a crew out to cover the story and it was on the six o'clock news tonight. Several people were interviewed—Andrea O'Shields and Laurie Hendrix were working triage and Laurie was interviewed. Both were on camera. We teased them about being TV stars and they promised to practice their 'celebrity wave.'

[At one of the worship services, Ramona Lewis is asked to preach]
We worshipped at the different churches all over town and three of our group were asked to preach. I was one of the three. That was a first-time experience for me, preaching and doing it through an interpreter. But I did the best I could and God doesn't ask for more than that. Right? Mac Lawton, Joe and Andrea O'Shields, Wanda

and Lorie King and I sang "Victory in Jesus" and "Blessed Assurance." We sounded pretty good, too!

[From the Message Board and Prayer Requests at First Baptist Church of Easley, this message is from Newton. It is edited because of problems in spelling]
My name is Newton..i was in this hotel that you are..i am friend of the girls, Toya, Sarah and other). I am writing to talk to you that I loved your work in brazil..thank's for people to help our country..if possible..you send me other email..and if Toya can speak something…Thanks.

The Pantavida Boat

Prayer service of 'mission' group from Easley Baptist Church

Chapter Forty-Three
Note from Ramona

Before typing Ramona's Note , I'd like to tell what a good friend she has been to Andrea and Joe O'Shields and her family. Ramona is a lovely and unique person; a joy to be around. In my family history, Andrea discovered a connection with Ramona's relatives and our Allen family. Andrea knew that I was doing research on the Allen family and that I had been fortunate to find and copy the work of Postell Allen. She asked me if I knew Pansy Allen. I said, "Yes, she was kind enough to allow me to copy the history Postell Allen had done!" Pansy and I talked on the phone and I learned she was the wife of Postell Allen, Jr. She told me she had a copy of Postell's research and would be happy for me to make copies from it. How nice she was! She didn't know me at all, but I told her that my father, Louis Allen and Postell Allen, Sr. were first cousins—their fathers were brothers and their grandfather was Reverend Jesse Allen. Andrea said she knew a lady in the church there in Easley, whose sister was Pansy Allen! Somehow I couldn't believe she was the same one who married Postell Allen, Jr.——But she was and guess whose sister Pansy Allen was? *It was Ramona Lewis!!!*

I knew Ramona's face and I had talked to her about the Allen family as we sat in the waiting room while granddaughter, Toya O'Shields had surgery for a broken ankle. This was in Palmetto Baptist Hospital, in Easley, SC. Ramona's husband was in the hospital at the time. This is the same hospital where Andrea is a nurse—working in the ER and in Intensive Care. We had seen each other at church functions but somehow when I read the Brazil 2001 Journal on the First Baptist Church of Easley's website, the Journalist's name, Ramona Lewis "didn't ring a bell."

I wrote Ramona and asked if she approved of my use of parts of her journal, in which the O'Shields' family were mentioned. To my chagrin, I realized after writing and expressing a wish to meet her—that I knew who she was!! I felt so stupid and told Andrea to apologize to her because I did know her but just didn't put the face with the name!

It is such a pleasure to include the following note from Ramona:

Mrs. Harvey,   Sept. 19, 2003

Please forgive me for taking so long to reply to your lovely request. I put it in a drawer on my desk and "out of sight, out of mind."

First of all, I am honored by your request. Use any of my writing That you want to include in your family history/journal and I will be in good company.

Secondly, I have met you twice, once at our church and most recently at Greer 1st Bapt. When our choirs sang "Feel the Spirit."

Thank you for your kind words about my mission journaling efforts. My fingers type the words but the Holy Spirit enables the composition.

By His Grace,
Ramona Lewis

Chapter Forty-Four
Reflections

In 1999, daughter, Beth Phillips was named teacher of the year at East Greer Elementary School. The year 2000 came and East Greer Elementary was closed; the new elementary school in Greer was Chandler Creek Elementary. Beth's husband David was continuing his work as organist and choir director at Trinity Methodist Church in Spartanburg, SC. Their daughter, Meryl, completed fourth grade at Crestview Elementary. She went camping with Kelsey Templeton and her family several times and enjoyed fishing and swimming! She was a great help cutting our grass on Bill's riding lawn mower.

Allison O'Shields graduated from Wren High School and Ashley O'Shields completed her freshman year at North Greenville College (2000). [Allison entered Clemson University in the fall, but transferred later to North Greenville College.] Toya O'Shields enjoyed fishing with her Dad; also, swimming and roller blade skating.

Brandon and Toya O'Shields had a good year in soccer. Brandon's team was in the soccer tournament. Brandon worked with his Dad putting in sprinkler systems in the summer and fall. He made excellent grades and so have all the other O'Shields' children. [When Brandon graduated from Wren High School, his total GPA was 4.627.]

My thanks to granddaughter, Allison O'Shields for the devotional/journal, Streams in the Desert. These notes and comments were taken from my writings in it. Speaking of Allison; she was perfect in the role of "Marcy" in the North Greenville production, "You're a Good Man Charlie Brown." I wrote also of the choral concerts at North Greenville (when Ashley and Allison were in the concert choir) and how wonderful Ashley's voice recitals were. [Today Ashley and Allison are student teaching and will graduate this spring (2004–Allison took summer courses, making this possible.]

From a journal I wrote these reflections of the years 2001,

2002 and 2003. As we start the New Year (2002) my thoughts go back to 2001 and all that happened. One important event was the high school graduation of grandson, Justin Harvey.

Another was our celebration June 26, 2001 of our Golden Wedding Anniversary. The family met at "the Peddlar" restaurant for our anniversary dinner. Before the meal, Andrea's photographer friend, Mary Lou Banks took our picture — a family portrait. It's on the wall in the den where we enjoy looking at it.

Andrea, Joe, Ashley, Allison, Brandon and Toya went again on mission trip to Corumba, Brazil.

Beth, David and Meryl became members of Our Saviour Lutheran Church (how nice for me—having family with me at church.) Meryl Phillips entered Greer Middle School and Amy Harvey; Greer High School.

Donna Harvey started working at Greer State Bank. Chris Harvey performed his first wedding! Amy Harvey and I went to "Judgment Hall" in October (Washington Baptist Church in Greenville) and the Art Museum at Bob Jones University in December.

September 7, 2001, Donna and I went to Mary's Restaurant in Fountain Inn (for her Birthday.) It was just four days before the Terrorist Attacks—- the Twin Towers in New York City and the Pentagon in Washington, D.C. It was the work of Ben Laden terrorists! The airports were shut down!! Three thousand lives were lost. The clean up continues at Ground Zero! [Today it is completed and a memorial is planned for the site.]

Christmas Eve day, Bill got a new pacemaker. We were at the hospital at 6:00 a.m. and the surgery was 8:45 a.m. All went well and we left the hospital at approximately 1:20 p.m. The family came for Christmas get-together that evening. Lots of fun! The food brought by Donna, Beth and Andrea was delicious! At one point of the evening, Justin played the guitar—a nice present!

197

Andrea gave me a CD of Paul Mauriat. She made the CD because she knew I loved his music—music we enjoyed listening to as we traveled together when Andrea was about nine; Chris, twelve and Beth, sixteen—another wonderful 'silver' memory! I tried to get Amy to line dance with me but Brandon did, instead—I'm not sure that appeals to his age group. Another present: David and Meryl at the piano with their rendering of two Christmas duets! Lovely!!!

Bill managed to sit up and be a part of all our noisemaking. Medication from the surgery and pain medicine carried him through the evening. Chris had surgery, himself, to remove a bone spur from his shoulder. His surgery was after Christmas—yesterday Donna called to say they were getting ready to come home. She said he was doing fine. We talked last night and he was still doing well.

As I reflect, I'm not sure if the year is 2001 or 2000, when Donna and Chris went to the Grand Canyon. It was a short trip won as a prize! A nice experience for them. Donna had never flown before but she didn't have any problems.

Aunt Julia Allen died this past December. She was the wife of Daddy's brother, Dr. Albert L. Allen., — a radiologist in Winchester, Kentucky. We visited them in 1969 (Bill, Beth, Chris, Andrea and I) and watched the Moon Landing, July 20th. We watched the television set as the Astronaut walked on the moon!

Our neighbor, Mrs. Leona Cox, celebrated her 102nd birthday this past October. On July 14th, (Beth's birthday) we went to another birthday celebration—the 70th birthday celebration of my childhood friend, Thelma Cooper Merritt.

This past summer, we also went to my 50th High School reunion at Greer High.

After Christmas, I went to a Drop-In Golden Wedding Anniversary for Pat and Ken Mullins. Pat has always been a dear friend—we go back to grammar school at Central Elementary in Greer. Pat was a bridesmaid for me and I was one for her. Other bridesmaids of Pat's were Alexander Taleff Crosland, Ruth Davis, Billie Hope Simmons, Dorothy Mason Bryson, Barbara Smith and Cleo Jones Skinner; her maid of honor. Other bridesmaids for me were Dot Mason Bryson, Francis Cannon Hester, Barbara Smith, Amy Smith Boozer, Peggy Jean Smith and maid of honor, Ann Johnston Cooper. [I have never been good about details and especially now that I'm older.]It was great seeing everyone—Cleo, Alexandra, Dot, Billie Hope, Linda, Pat, Kenneth and their children Michael and Lee Ann. Dot commented how nice my grandson, Justin is. She said she enjoyed talking to him when he worked for Quality Foods in Greer.

Jan. 21, 2002: I celebrated another birthday yesterday (69 years). Andrea had a dinner for me on the 19th—a wonderful meal and lovely time! Chris had a sinus infection and Justin was working so they were not there but Beth, David and Meryl and Andrea's family were. Some of us watched "Pearl Harbor" (video upstairs) and others played pool downstairs. Toya showed me her sketches. She must be artistic! She drew a 'life-size' picture of an angel on her bedroom wall! In spite of having 'mono', she kept up her grades—even making 102 grade points in science!

After the movie, we had cake (my birthday cake, saying Happy Birthday, Toya.) Everyone sang Happy Birthday to Mama, Toya, and Grandmama—it was neat hearing the different names sung at the same time! Andrea had only about three hours of sleep, she worked the night before (Palmetto Baptist Hospital, Easley, SC.) I believe she'll have 102 points racked up in heaven! May God give her strength and health on her journey!

Sunday, Jan. 20th: To church with Beth, we sat with Sadie Dominick and Nancy Nix. Outside we visited with Harriet and Lee Smyre. Beth and I left right after communion. We came back and picked up Meryl. She had stayed with Bill because of bad cold. Bill said she slept while we were gone. Beth, Meryl and I went to Converse College Dining Room in Spartanburg, where David was playing the piano for "brunch." The manager told us to go on in— it was on the house! He wished me Happy Birthday! So did three other workers. One named Burt, met us and took us to our table. The music David played was especially nice!! The atmosphere was traditional—tablecloths and linen napkins. The buffet was attractively appointed. I was given a Red Rose.

Chris and Donna came by in the late afternoon. They gave me a lovely card with money inside! We had a nice visit. Justin was at work but I did see him on Friday (Jan. 18th) at Praise Cathedral. The Emergency NYPD workers came to Greer and Justin was there, as was Chris. I got over to see Justin and gave him a hug before I left.

Feb. 18, 2002: Many family birthdays this year—Justin Harvey (Jan. (9th), and Brandon O'Shields (Jan. 26th). Justin turned 19 and Brandon, 17. February 7th, Ashley O'Shields had her 21st birthday. She and I went shopping and on to a sandwich shop on Augusta Road in Greenville. Her friend Erika, works there. We had Cappucino's with our food. Erika brought out a chocolate mousse for Ashley's birthday surprise! The entire meal was free! Erika and her boss wouldn't let us pay.

Bill's birthday was Feb. 13th. I bought a TCBY ice cream cake for him. Beth and Meryl were here earlier; Chris, Donna and Amy came later.

For Chris's birthday Nov. 26th we went to Fatz and he was given a 'special' dessert and wished Happy Birthday by the staff.

Amy Harvey and Toya O'Shields enjoyed their birthdays, yesterday, Feb. 17th. Amy had friends over for a sleep-over. Toya's birthday was celebrated at Myabi's Restaurant in Greenville, with family. Amy was sixteen; Toya was fifteen.

This weekend Chris was allowed to keep and drive a BMW Z3 automobile. It was a promotional 'deal' arranged by the city administrator.

Bill's sister, Jean came by on Bill's birthday. She seemed to be doing well. We went to pick up Meryl at Greer Middle School. [Jean died Feb. 4, 2003]

Meryl started a class that will prepare her for taking communion in our church. She with others will take communion at the Maunday Thursday Service at church.

Our new Pastor, Reverend Gerald Smith, held his first service yesterday. A good, dedicated man with a strong speaking voice; he brings energy and enthusiasm and devotion to his job as Pastor.

Bill was carried to the hospital in Greenville Monday, Mar. 24, 2002. Because of Chest pain and shortness of breath, a stress test was done; today heart catherization. Minor blockages were found but the more serious problem: the inability of the heart to pump as it should. It only pumps 20 to 35% of what it should. Two new medications started: Lanoxin and Toprol.

This is the same day the President comes to Greenville, SC. The firefighters and fire chiefs in this area were invited to hear the President speak. Chris was in Greenville around 5:00 a.m. WYFF news coverage was presented on the 6:00 news and we saw Chris and the firemen and President Bush on TV. Chris actually stood beside the President and shook his hand. A picture was made [I have it on my computer today.]

Bill came home from the hospital, Friday Mar. 28th. This coming Sunday is Easter.

[Forward to December 2002.] December 29, 2002: A memorable day began with the 11:00 church service at Our Saviour Lutheran Church. Granddaughter, Ashley O'Shields sang solo, "Lullaby" during the service. Andrea, Joe, Brandon, Toya and friend, Bridgett came to the service [Allison was sick with a sore throat and cold.] All of us sat together directly behind Beth, Meryl and our friend, Sadie Dominick. The church still decked out from Christmas, was beautiful—two

Chrismon trees and many, many poinsettias arranged up to a point, like a Christmas tree. Ashley's solo was lovely! I told her I felt she was singing it just for me. Actually, she received a monetary gift for singing.

December 26, 2002: My friend, Helen yost died of chronic Leukemia. She managed her illness well. Our friendship began at Redeemer Lutheran in Greet, SC. In this mission church (actually a Small house) everyone pulled together and made the services unique! Pastor James Addy, along with his wife Cely, were instrumental in establishing the church—the first Lutheran Church in Greer, SC. Pastor Addy anounced plans to relocate with this family to another Pastorate in Charleston, SC and our family became Lutheran except son, Chris who remained a Presbyterian until he married a Baptist!

February 15, 2002: Birthday party for the "February" people in our family—Bill, Ashley, Amy, and Toya. All their names were on the cake. All the family came and brought food. We played the game, Cranium—pretty hard for this Grand Mother.

Bill has been confined at home for all of February. He wasn't able to attend his sister, Jean's funeral or Justin's graduation and party. Bill doesn't complain, but I know it hurts when he can't be a part of everything. As I write, he is in the back bedroom, watching and listening to the "Gaither's" on television. The group is singing "The Haven of Rest"—'with Jesus I'm safe, evermore.'

Family get-together in Cleveland Park, Greenville, SC
All the immediate Harvey family except David Phillips,
Beth's husband. The photographer: my cousin Steve Connelly.
His son, Tom Connelly is standing in front of me
with my arm over his shoulder.

The 'Golden Group'
The picture was made by friend nancy Riskevics at "The
Junction" above Greer near Highway 11. From left: Toya
Harvey, next Gloria Pruett (Queen of the Impossible) followed
by Mary Counts [neighboring pew buddy] and 'the Miracle
Lady,' Mary Ann Copenhaver; it is a miracle she is alive!

Chapter Forty-Five

Opening Prayer
December 15, 2003
WELCA Bible Study

Lutheran Church of Our Saviour

In a spirit of thanksgiving to God for the pleasure of His Company; we pray for any who might have concerns about their faith. Please hear the prayers of all who need healing and comfort and for those who face problems in work or family situations. May there always be those believers who are willing to be examples for others to imitate. Help us to conduct ourselves in holiness and honor—even in our most difficult moments. And now Lord, we thank you for the pleasure of being in this company of believers today. Let us conclude this prayer by saying to each other: I thank God for the pleasure of your company.

Amen

A highlight of the Christmas season 2003 was a WELCA luncheon at the home of member, Geneva Larson. A delightful meal and Christian fellowship followed the Bible study. Geneva's lovely home sits high in the mountains overlooking Greer and Spartanburg.

Jenny Simmons, Joan Bjork and I were chauffeured by Dorothy Rimer. Lois Kemp also drove, accompanied by Betty Buckwell. Our president, Geneva Ring was unable to be with us; she was recovering from dental surgery.

It was my privilege to lead the study of the book of lst Thessalonians and to give the benediction from lst Thessalonians 5:23. The benediction is one used by many ministers. It was often used by Reverend John K. Johnston at First Presbyterian Church in Greer at the time my family and I were members there. May it be as meaningful to you, Reader—as it has been to me.

Now may the God of peace Himself

Santify you completely; and may

Your whole spirit, soul, and body

Be preserved blameless at the

Coming of our Lord Jesus Christ.

1 Thessalonians 5:23

The Lutheran Church of our Saviour
Greenville, South Carolina

Chapter Forty-Six
Spring 2004

The Lutheran Church of Our Saviour (Greenville, SC) observed Palm Sunday April 4, 2004. Pastor Jerry Smith, the Crucifer, Torch Bearers and Accolyte began the processional, followed by the congregation into the church. This was the 8:30 service and the weather was cold and windy. Granddaughter Meryl Phillips was one of the two torch bearers. Upon entering the church, members were given handmade crosses and palm branches. Potted palms surrounded the altar. Meryl's participation and smile as she recessed out at the end of the service added to the special day—especially for her mother, Beth and me.

That same Sunday, I attended a service—a musical worship service presented by the choir of Locust Hill Baptist Church. This church has been helpful and caring to many of the students from North Greenville College. They have been supportive and inviting to our granddaughters, Ashley and Allison O'Shields by welcoming them into their church and into the choir.

The Sanctuary Choir presented "Like a Lamb" by Camp Kirkland. Ashley and Allison both had solos—Allison sang 'Love Would Cost the Highest Price,' and Ashley sang 'Arms Wide Open.' I always knew Allison was musical, had a great voice and could sing—but I just didn't realize how good she was!! She just 'blew me away' with her soulful magic! I thought as I listened, "it can't get any better than this" —and then it was Ashley's turn. Well, she just brought the house down!! Being a voice major, and being trained as a coloratura soprano, she certainly has operatic potential; in fact Ashley will start her graduate studies in voice this fall at the University of Southern Mississippi [Ashley is in her second year of graduate studies, September 2005]and Allison will be teaching fourth grade in the public school system in South Carolina [Allison married Brian Cawley and is living in Spartanburg and teaching 5th grade in the Spartanburg County School system, September 2005.] These sisters complement each other, not only in their singing but also with their own unique personalities.

The North Greenville College graduation ceremony is May 6, 2004. A cook-out celebration is planned by Andrea and Joe O'Shields on May 1, 2004. With Daughter-in-law, Donna Harvey and granddaughter, Amy Harvey, I am planning a family dinner at our home after the graduation. This will not be the only graduation ceremony to celebrate this year! Granddaughter, Amy Harvey graduates from Greer High School June 4, 2004. Amy and two of her fellow classmates and friends are having a graduation party given by their parents at Victor Baptist Fellowship Hall.

Just three days after Amy's graduation, she will be leaving on a tour with a group from Greer High School to visit Paris, Munich and Switzerland. What an opportunity for Amy and for 'yours truly'—yes, I'm going too!! We will depart from Charlotte, NC at 4:30 p.m. and arrive (their time) 7:00 a.m. in Frankfort, Germany. (I think our daughter Andrea did the same departure and arrival when she went to France with French Class from Greer High, but their itinerary included Spain also.) I look forward to traveling with Amy but I'll leave with mixed feelings. My dear grandchildren—what would I do with out them? Ashley and Allison have agreed to stay with Bill while I'm gone and Donna and Chris will check on Bill during noontime every day.

Summer will pass quickly for Chris and Donna and Amy. They will be going to New Orleans in August and Amy will start to Winthrop University in Rock Hill at the end of August. Justin, Amy's brother has relocated to another fire department—Wade Hampton at East North Street in Greenville, SC. He likes it very much but stays busy. Justin has adjusted well to the demands of a firefighter. We commend him and all firefighters.

Brandon O'Shields is transferring to Anderson College from Clemson University as a sophomore [September 2005, he is now a junior.] Always a good student, he originally intended to major in business administration but now he is considering taking courses in preparation for youth ministry. He is such a believer and grand person, whatever Brandon chooses will benefit others—he has always put others first. When he and his sisters were younger, we'd take them shopping and Brandon would look for items for the girls or for me or for Bill, but not for himself.

Toya O'Shields has worked as a waitress this year and so has Amy Harvey. Toya will be a Senior at Wren High School (Anderson District 1) {Toya graduated from Wren and is now a freshman at Anderson College, Anderson, Indiana.} Meryl Phillips will enter ninth grade at Greer High School{Meryl is now in 10th grade at Byrnes High School, September 2005}. Toya and all of her family will be going to Williamsburg, VA the last of May 2004. I know it will be a good trip and a great time for all. Meryl and her mom and dad, Beth and David Phillips will be going to the beach, I believe—if not Meryl will go with her friend Brandi Vaughn and her family. Meryl and Brandi are in the same grade and both are clarinet players in the school band. The Spring Concert is tomorrow night, Thursday April 29, 2004. I'm going with Beth and David.

June 2004
Trip to Germany Switzerland and Paris

"Bon Voyage!" "We're leaving Charlotte at 4:30 p.m. and will be back on June 16th." These were my words I emailed my cousin, Steve Connelly. Here is a short summary of how and why I broke away from the normal day-to-day routine in Greer, SC in June 2004.

Granddaughter, Amy Harvey and her senior class of Greer High School were planning a trip to Europe with ACIS Travel Group and teacher/leader Tracy Miller. Adults, especially grandparents were invited to travel with the group. It seemed like a dream that I might be able to go!! I began to make plans for someone to stay with Bill and to learn all about his medications. My oldest granddaughter Ashley O'Shields volunteered. She and her sister, Allison graduated from North Greenville College in May 2004. Even though Ashley was the 'nurse' while I was gone, other family members helped— as well as friend, Sarrell Strange who stayed with Bill several nights. Since Ashley would take time off from her job as waitress at 'Red Lobster,' we agreed on a salary that would be compatible with her earnings as waitress. Ashley was an excellent nurse!! I needn't have worried about Bill—He enjoyed the company and the attention!

Bill and friend, Sarrell visited Bradshaw Automobile Dealership the day of my arrival home. In fact, with Sarrell's assistance, he purchased a Hyundai SUV! Since Bill had not been driving before I left, this was a complete shock when I heard the news from my son, Chris. Chris and Donna,, Amy's parents, picked us up at the Charlotte Airport after our flight home. Hearing the news, I felt as though someone had knocked my feet out from under me!

The following Sunday at church, our pastor, Pastor Jerry [Rev. Gerald Smith, Lutheran Church of Our Saviour] asked about the trip and how Bill was. "Bill's full of surprises," was my answer and I explained what I meant. I am glad that Bill traded in his Mazda truck. Our son-in-law Joe O'Shields and grandson, Brandon (not to mention Andrea our daughter and Chris our son) had done everything possible to get the Mazda running again. Chris had put in a new gas line, but something kept going wrong. It was time for the Mazda 'to go.'

Another story concerning the Mazda and Bill's 'surprises' but this time Bill was on the receiving end of the surprise! Bill had a friend who painted the Mazda. He was a truck painting specialist who wanted someone to invest in his business. Of course Bill was taken in and provided the money! This money was never returned. Naturally I was affected but there was nothing we could do. So what do you do when life hands you a lemon? Make lemonade. I have a plaque which says it all: "Thou Shalt Not Whine."

We have to remember the tragic circumstances that are handled bravely and gracefully every day. What is the quote? "Help me to change the things that need to be changed and to accept the things which cannot be changed—and the wisdom to know the difference."

ICIS Travel Group 2004
Back row, far right: Toya Harvey
Front row, far right: Amy Harvey

Chapter Forty-Seven
What I've Learned from My Children and Grandchildren

When all the grandchildren were small, it was a treat when they came to visit! I served them hot tea with milk and sugar, and raisin bread toast. They liked to sit at a folding step stool which opened up to a 'sort of table.' The lower step became a seat and the upper step was a ledge to hold their food. So many memories! Bill and I had such joy as we became children with them! Many times we took them places—Now our roles are being reversed; instead, we are the ones being taken.

What have I learned from my children and grandchildren? From Andrea's four, I've learned not to take life so seriously—from their example I've realized that situations need not be perfect to be enjoyed. From the Harvey grandchildren, I've learned to be your own person, regardless of 'peer pressure.' From Meryl Phillips, I've learned that by showing vulnerability you expose yourself to being hurt by others but also you open yourself to new experiences and nice surprises if you're willing to take the risk.

From my children, I've learned how disciplined they are! I admire the strong work ethic each one has. I see how they face their obligations of work and family—regardless of the stress involved!

Our oldest, Beth teaches first grade and aside from the teaching aspect, she spends many hours planning lessons, grading papers, arranging conferences with parents, working bus duty, attending teachers' meetings and PTA meetings and working after school. She rarely ever takes any sick leave. [written before Beth retired from teaching [2004] in the Greenville County public school system—she now is a teacher for kindergarten in Our Saviour Lutheran Day School, September 2005.

Our middle child, Christopher has many responsibilities as Fire Chief of the Greer Fire Department. Aside from his duties as Fire Chief, he is called upon to attend council meetings and numerous city meetings and functions affecting the city of Greer. I'm sure that I and others are not aware of how active he must be in the community of Greer. Often called upon to take part in community activities, he has been a speaker at different churches and in classes of Greer High School and Elementary Schools of Greer. This year [2004] he gave the devotional for Greer High students in the Greer Release Time Program. There is so much he is involved with and does – (this could be another book.)

Our youngest, Andrea doesn't shirk her responsibilities either! A nurse at Palmetto Baptist Hospital in Easley, SC, Andrea works in the Emergency Room or in the Intensive Care Unit—as she says wherever she's needed. Usually working 12-hour night shifts for at least three nights a week; sometimes more. She often adds a day shift here and there. Meeting the demands of home, work and church, she regularly attended soccer matches when Brandon and Toya had games, as well as school events, concerts, etc., the children were involved in. She continually does a balancing act that would be hard to follow!

Beth, Chris and Andrea have been conscientious in their roles of service—in work and family. They also have been a strong support to Bill and me throughout the years. I can never find the words to express how much their support has meant to me! That is what 'family' means isn't it? Let me also thank my sons-in-law, Joe O'Shields and David Phillips and daughter-in-law, Donna Harvey for their kindness, love and concern.

Phillips: David, Beth and Meryl

BETH PHILLIPS (CO-TOY)
First Grade
Chandler Creek Elementary

Beth Phillips, Teacher of the Year 1999-2000

Meryl Phillips 2005

214

Chapter Forty-Eight
Update 2005

I have finally decided to publish. My goal is to have all ready by October lst. Choosing Lifevest Publishers gives me the incentive to finish my part of this family tapestry.

On July 9, 2005, another extension was added to the family. Granddaughter, Allison O'Shields married a fine young man, Brian Cawley! The wedding took place at Easley Baptist Church, Easley, SC. This wedding is a <u>first</u>—the first grandchild to marry and the first of Andrea and Joe O'Shields' children to marry. In fact, when Toya O'Shields leaves for college, August 24, 2005 (Anderson College, Indiana) all the O'Shields' siblings will be leaving the nest. Ashley O'Shields will be completing work on her masters and Brandon O'Shields will be a junior at Anderson College, Anderson, SC.

Many thoughts entered my mind the day of the wedding. As I took Brandon's arm and he escorted me down the aisle (for the seating of the grandparents) I thought how beautiful Allison was (I had already seen her in her wedding gown), how handsome Brandon and the ushers were and how lovely the bridesmaids and maid of honor were—Toya was one of the bridesmaids and Ashley was the maid of honor—and how precious the flower girls were— in their long white dresses scattering white rose petals from their flower baskets! Lest I forget, let me remember the stunning parents, Andrea and Joe O'Shields and the groom's mother and step-father, Sandy and Ron Bartlett. After I was seated, Bill was escorted down in a wheelchair while the pianist Rick Roe played "Tis a Gift to be Simple, Tis a Gift to be Free."

My, how the times, are a-changing! Our son's daughter, granddaughter Amy Harvey is now in her sophomore year at Winthrop University. She and other suitemates have leased an

215

apartment. Amy and I did some shopping this summer at thrift stores where she found some good buys. This happened before when Ashley was getting ready to go to Mississippi. Ashley and I also looked for items for the duplex she and another girlfriend share in Mississippi.

Meryl Phillips, another granddaughter is changing high schools. She will be a 10th grader at Brynes High (Spartanburg Co, SC). Meryl's summer has been filled with church activities— Lutheran youth convention in Newberry, SC; Camp HUGG for disabled children, Lexington, SC; and a mission trip to Key West, FLA. Now that she has her driver's permit, she chauffeurs her granddaddy quite often. Her mother, Beth Phillips, retired from teaching in the public school system in June 2005; however, she will be teaching Kindergarten at Lutheran Church of Our Saviour Day School. Beth's schedule will be much lighter—8:30 -12:00. Now Meryl will know how it feels for her mother to pick her up from school—something she has missed.

Speaking of firsts—grandson Justin Harvey has taken up a new instrument in addition to the guitar—the banjo—playing with some group players when he's not 'pulling a shift' at the Wade Hampton Fire Department.

Toya O'Shields flew solo to the Florida keys to spend time with friends. She was in Florida when Allison O'Shields was honoree at a bridal shower given by Beth and Meryl Phillips; Donna and Amy Harvey. The location: home of Toya Harvey. Refreshments: decorated cake and delicious strawberries with dip and sausage balls plus punch, cookies and nuts. [Did I forget anything?] Meryl Phillips served as 'roving' photographer. Many of Allison's friends and relatives came as did her future mother-in-law Sandy Bartlett. Brian Cawley, Allison's fiancée and his step-father Ron Bartlett were in the den chatting. The bridal shower was in living room. Brian and his parents drove from Aiken, where his parents live.

Earlier in the summer, a bridal luncheon took place at the home of Barbara Welmaker in Easley. It was a Choir member luncheon made up of sopranos of whom Allison, Ashley and Andrea O'Shields were members. Toya O'Shields was there, as well. [Andrea is still a member and has been since the girls were toddlers.] How nice for this mother and grandmother to be included among the guests! A place setting of stainless flatware was presented to Allison by the hostesses. These ladies were gracious in their hospitality and the delightful meal appreciated by all.

Ashley is back in Mississippi at the University of Mississippi and Allison is living in Spartanburg, SC. Toya is in Anderson, Indiana—a freshman at Anderson College.

Two weeks before Allison's wedding, Andrea and son Brandon O'Shields flew to Montana to take part in a church sponsored [Easley Baptist] sports camp. Allison would comment often, "Can you believe she's (Andrea) doing this two weeks before my wedding?" Certainly when Andrea and Brandon returned there was much to do. I can't begin to name all that needed to be done. Decorating the church, especially the fellowship hall where tables were set up and a catered buffet served after the wedding. On the day of the wedding, Andrea invited the bridesmaids to a wedding brunch for Allison. I'm sure all the O'Shields 'pitched in' and helped but Andrea did the cooking.

A short time after the wedding, the last of August 2005, Andrea, Joe and Toya would be taking two vehicles: Toya in her car; Joe and Andrea in his truck, towing a trailer which included 39 pairs of Toya's shoes! Before Toya and her parents left, two events took place: August 16th, Bill Harvey was admitted to Greenville Memorial Hospital with pneumonia. He stayed for a week and ran fever for five straight days. I slept on chair that opened into a cot in his room for those five days. His pneumonia spread to both lungs. He came home August 23rd. It seems the next event, Hurricane Katrina occurred in that time span. Because I was up during the nights I stayed with Bill, the hurricane and Bill's hospitalization seem to run together. I must remember, even though the weather reports were saying Katrina was on the way; that it would probably hit New Orleans and Gulfport, Biloxi and Mobile—the Gulf coast from Louisiana, Mississippi and Alabama. Bill did come home before Katrina hit New Orleans—August 28th, 29th. What a catastrophe!!!

The flooding of New Orleans left people stranded without food or water for days; evacuees moved into other states; rescue efforts were made by the Coast Guard, the military and the national guard—not to mention the firemen and policemen brought in from out of state; lives were lost; homes destroyed; entire parishes demolished. The destruction and chaos cannot be accurately described—someone said on TV that the area Katrina hit was the size of Great Britain! Future generations will read about Katrina in History Books!

Granddaughter Ashley O'Shields left with Mary Chung from Hattiesburg, MS. They went to Jackson, MS and stayed with a fellow student's family there. There was no electricity and no stores were open except a WalMart and one filling station. To get into WalMart or the filling station required at least a two hour wait! When the situation became worse in New Orleans and Biloxi, Mary and Ashley came on to South Carolina. After about two weeks, the college, the University of Southern Mississippi, reopened and Ashley returned to USM. The duplex where Ashley and her roommate lived was not damaged except for some tiles blown off the roof.

[Here follows an article taken from a newsletter from "The Sanctuary Choir," First Baptist Church, Easley, SC May 4, 2005] A picture of Ashley O'Shields, in the company of Placido Domingo and I assume, Anna Maria Martinez –Ashley is on the right, Placido Domingo is in the middle and Anna Maria Martinez on the left. The Caption reads:

218

NAME THAT FAMOUS MUSICIAN!

It's Ashley O'Shields! That's right. Ashley is the one standing next to Placido Domingo. Here's Ashley in her own words…"Hi! I am closing out my first Year of graduate school and I'm ready for a break. On April 2 Placido Domingo came to Mississippi for a concert sponsored by USM. Our own orchestra played for him. About 11,000 people were in attendance that evening. Placido was incredible; he still sounds great in his old age. Anna Maria Martinez was the guest soprano for the evening. I was able to go to the VIP reception after the concert. WOW!!! I spoke with him for a little while and he is such a nice man. I am amazed at the opportunities I have been given. I have attached a few pictures from the reception. In February the choir I sing in, sang at the National ACDA convention in Los Angeles, CA. I got to hear the St. Olaff choir and Mormon Tabernacle choir sing in LA. I have learned a lot this year and look forward to another great year."

Granddaughter Ashley O'Shields.
She is to the right of Placido Domingo.

We received this card from Ashley recently.

Hi,

I wanted to take time out of my busy schedule to tell you "thanks" for being such great, supporting grandparents. I have always been able to happily tell people that I have such loving grandparents. You have been a positive impact on the woman I am today. Thanks for helping steer me in the right direction. I am going to try to call more often. I hope you both have a wonderful grandparents day!!! I love you!!

Ashley

"Keeping in Touch on Grandparents Day"

Taking time out
To keep in touch—
And let you know
You mean so much

As this family record draws to a close, the story still continues, evolving into a never ending but everlasting spiral. The miracles of life on earth will spiral into miracles of eternal life.

Harvey, Bill and Toya
Andrea, Chris, Beth

Petting Zoo? Greer Fire Chief Chris Harvey arrived to work on Monday to find the headquarters station transformed into a pink flamingo petting zoo. The fire department made the list of numerous yards being flocked by teens from Greer First Presbyterian Church raising funds for their summer mission trip.

Students at Chandler Creek Elementary celebrate Hat Day. Teacher Beth Phillips, in back, with students, front row from left, Jesse Michael, Courtney Newman, Michael Shell and Destiny Hawkins. Back row: Kyle Johnson, Trey Adams, Caleb Sanchez and Christy Walker.

Appendix of Surnames

Surnames of Wales and England

Under the 'Surnames of Wales' page 191 of the <u>Celtic Book of Names</u>, is the name, "Awbrey,'—remember ancestor, Louisa de Aubrey Tucker? Someone in our Welsh ancestry was named 'Awbrey' or 'Aubrey.' Since the middle name of Louisa Tucker is de Aubrey, it certainly adds French color to the Welsh name. This name is spoken of as a Welsh adaptation of the surname, de Alberico—a Norman surname that appeared in Wales shortly after the Norman conquest. It is concentrated in Glamorgan and south Wales; variants are Aubrey and Obray." (Conway, D.J.)

On page 215 of 'Surnames of Wales' is the name, 'Tucker.' "This surname comes from an English occupational name, which means 'one who fulls cloth.' This surname is inter-changeable with the name, 'Fuller.' Found in the southern parts of Wales, the areas that were subjected to the greatest English influence." (Ibid.)

Also from the same source of surnames by Conway, a statement is made referring to 'Allen' as an English name: "This English surname was brought into Britain with the Norman invaders and comes from the personal name, Alan. By 1853, this name was quite common in both England and Wales." (191.)

From the internet, under <u>Irish Ancestors/Surnames</u> is a short history of the 'Allen' name: Allen has two quite distinct origins, one Scots-Gaelic, the other French. 'Allin,' meaning, 'little rock,' is the root of the Scottish name, originally MacAllan. The first recorded arrivals bearing the Scottish name came in the fifteenth century as hired soldiers ('gallowglasses') imported to Donegal by the O'Donnells, and the migrations of the following two centuries brought more.

In other cases, the surname derives from the Old Breton personal name Alan, which in which in turn came from the Germanic tribal name Alemannus, meaning 'all men.' The same root provided the modern French name for Germany, Allemagne. Followers of the invading Normans were the first to carry the Breton version of the name to Ireland. Irish families bearing the name may be of either origin, though the fact that two-thirds of the Allens are to be found in Ulster—(they are especially numerous in the counties of Antrim and Armagh) suggests that the majority are of the Scottish extraction.

Surname Associations in Scotland

Jardine

My grandfather League's sister was named Katie Jardine League. As already mentioned, the Leagues were French Huguenots who left France because of the revocation of the Edict of Nantes. My grandfather's mother, Annie Isabelle Creighton was of Scot ancestry. It is of interest that she chose the name, Jardine for her daughter.

From a web site on the internet, A HISTORY OF CLAN JARDINE approved by the Standing Council of Scottish Chiefs, I learned:

The name is derived from the French 'jardine' meaning garden. The family of du Jardon came over to England with William the Conqueror in 1066.

The chiefly line seems to have been established in the 14th century at Applegirth on the River Annan in Dumfriesshire. Their earliest stronghold was Spedlings Tower, which was later abandoned in favour of Jardine Hall. Sir Alexander Jardine of Applegirth was active in defending the Borders against the English.

From the Celtic Book of Names of Scotland, "At the Battle of Hastings, this name is listed as du Jardin. The family settled first near Kendal in the twelth century, then moved to Lanarkshire in the thirteenth century. Finally they settled in Dumfriesshire early in the fourteenth century. (Conway, 1999. p.175.)

Surname Associations in Scotland

Crichton

From A HISTORY OF CLAN CRICHTON, approved by the Standing Council of Scottish Chiefs: The lands of Kreitton formed one of the earliest baronies around Edinburgh and are mentioned in charters of the early 12th century.

Thurston de Crechtune was a witness to the foundation of the abbey of Holyrood House by David I in 1128. Thomas de Crichton swore fealty to Edward I of England in the Ragman Roll of 1296. Thomas had three sons each of whom extended the family holdings. William, his second son, married Isabel de Ross; heiress to the barony of Sanquhar in Dumfriesshire.

A descendant of his, Sir Robert Chrichton of Sanquhar, was sheriff of Dumfries in 1464.

Sir William Chrichton, another descendant of Thomas de Chrischton was chancellor of Scotland during the minority of James II.

The 2nd Lord Chrichton obtained through marriage the barony of Frendraught in Banfshire.

The 3rd Lord Chrichton joined the Duke of Albany in his rebellion against his royal brother James III. The rebellion failed and the Crichton estates were forfeited for treason.

Perhaps the most celebrated Crichton was James, son of the Lord Advocate of Scotland during the reigns of both Queen Mary and her son, James VI. He has passed into history as the Admiral Chrichton, on account of his superb mental and physical prowess.

Surname Associations of Scotland

MacQueen

The internet gives a brief history of the CLAN MAC-QUEEN approved by the Standing Council of Scottish Chiefs. This short history is not a history of the name MacQueen but rather of the Clan MacQueen. Therefore, some of the information may seem irrelevant; yet something may be gained from it that will strengthen the Allen/McQueen connection:

This Celtic name is also given as 'macSween,' or son of Sweyn. They are accordingly the same descent as the great Clan Donald, claiming kinship with the Irish High Kings.

The MacQueens are said to have provided a guard for a daughter of the house of Clan Ranald who married a MacKintosh chief, and they elected to settle around Findhorn and became part of that confederation of clans known as the Clans of the Cat, or Clan Catten.

The MacQueens were numerous throughout the islands. The Reverend Donald MacQueen, minister of Snizort, was a man of such intellect that he even impressed the great Dr. Samuel Johnson, who met him on his visit to the Hebrides.

My Family Fabric
Bibliography

Allen, Postell. Personal Interview with Mr. Andrew McHugh and Mr. B. A. McClimon. 11 Feb. 1941.

Bainbridge, Judith. "Conestee was early center of Greenville Industry." Greenville News 28 Aug. 2002.

Batson, Mann. A History of the Upper Part of Greenville County. Taylors: Faith Printing Co., 1993.

Bentley, James, and Anne Midgette. "Scotland." Nelles Guide. 1997.

"Battle of Hastings." Brittania's Homepage. 30 Sep. 2002. http://www.insurenet.co. uk/users/1066/ad/>.

Brown, Richard Maxwell. The South Carolina Regulators. Cambridge: Belknap Press of Harvard University Press. 1963.

Burch, Leland, ed., "Abner Creek Church Plans Sesquicentennial Celebration This Year." Greer: The Greer Citizen. 21 July 1982.

Cambrensis, Giraldus. " Book of Kells." British Columbia Library. 21 Apr. 2003 http://library.ubc.

"Clan Chrichton - A History of Clan Chrichton. " Approved by the Standing Council of Scottish Chiefs. 27 July 2002 <http://www.impressions.uk.com/clans/clan-27.shtml>.

"Clan Jardine – A History of Clan Jardine." Approved by the Standing Council of Scottish Chiefs. 27 July 2002 <http://www.impressions.uk.com/clans/clan-50.shtml>.

"Clan MacQueen – A History of Clan MacQueen." Approved by the Standing Council of. Scottish Chiefs. 27 July 2002 http://www.impressions.uk.com/clans/clan-137.shtml>.

Coleman and Givens. History of Fountain Inn.

Conway, D.J. The Celtic Book of Names. Secaucus: Carol Publishing Co., 1999.

Crenshaw, Rev. Bryan. "Homecoming, Dinner on Grounds was Great." The GreenvilleNews 1 May 1994.

Dobbs. History of Irish Trade (quoted by Lineham in Irish Scots and the Scotch-Irish) Dublin: 1727.

Duffy, Kevin. Who Were Those Celts? Bowie: Heritage Books, Inc. 1996.

Gates, Robert Cady. "Gates Family Forum." Online Posting. 18 Nov. 1999.

Glen, James. "A Description of the Province of South Carolina." SC Information Hwy. 2003.

Green, Mays League. "League Family History." Unpublished. Compiled and typed by Mrs. Annie Stenhouse: Greenville County 1980.

Harvey, Christopher Allen. "Personal Touch Made Frierson's Special." Greer Citizen 12 April 2000.

Henderson, Edna. Personal communication to Toya Harvey, 17 Oct. 1997.

Hipps, Frank. Memories of Old Simpsonville. Greenville: Express Press of Greenville. 1996.

Hitz, Alex M. Georgia Militia Districts, Reprint from GeorgiaBar Journal, vol. 18. no. 3. Atlanta: Ben W. Fortner Jr., Secy. of State. 1956.

Holcomb, Brent. Marriages and Death Notices from Baptist Newspapers of SC, vol. 1.

"Iron Age." Greenville News – Piedmont. Greenville: 11 Aug. 1985.

Jones, Lewis P. SC, A Synoptic History for Laymen. Orangeburg: Sandlapper   Publishing co. Inc. 1978.

Kennedy, Billy. The Scots – Irish in the Carolinas. Northern Ireland: Causeway Press   1997.

Landrum, John B.O. History of Spartanburg County. Spartanburg: Spartanburg Journal 1954.

Lester, Memory Aldrich. Old Southern Bible Records. Online posting by Robert Cady Gate's concerning this publication: Genealogical Publishing Co. 1974.

Lewis, Ramona. "Brazil 2001, Journal." First Baptist Church of Easley, Brazil Website.

Personal communication to Toya Harvey, 19 September 2003.

Lineham, John C. Irish Scots and the Scotch – Irish. Bowie: Heritage Books 1997.

Magnusson, Magnus. Landlord or Tenant. London: The Budley Head, 1978.

Mariboe, Knud. Encyclopedia of the Celts: http://celt.net/Celtic/celtopedia/t.html. 1994.

Morgan, Mike. "Gates Family Forum." Online posting: 18 Nov. 1999.

Morrison, Samuel Eliot. Oxford History of the American People vol. 1. New York: Oxford University Press 1972.

Olson, Marie Keenan. Personal communications to Toya Harvey 10th and 19th July 1999.

Obituary of Rev. Jesse Allen. Minutes of the Spartanburg Baptist Association, 1876-1895. Furman University Library. Greenville, SC.

O'Shields, Allison. " I Know Why the Grass is Green." Storm Front, a Wren High School Publication: Piedmont, S.C. 1998.

Perry, Tim, and Lisa Gerard-Sharp. Eyewitness Travel Guides – Ireland. New York: Doring Kindersley Publishing Co. 1997.

Phillips, Meryl. "My Interview with Toya Harvey." Unpublished Assignment – Greer Middle School, Greer, S.C. 2001.

Quennell, C.H.B. and Marjorie. Everyday Life in Roman and Anglo-Saxon Time New York: G.P. Putnam's Sons 1951.

Rogers,Virgil. Rogers – McCravy – Lanham. Strasburg: Shenandoah Publishing House, Inc. 1975.

Skinner, Mary Lee Barnett. James Calvin Skinner and Martha Elizabeth Gates Family Record. Edited by Lynwood Deal Jordan, Sr. Spartanburg: Copies, Ltd. 1987.

Stevenson, Robert Louis. "What Man May Learn, What Man May Do"<http://www.Poetryloverspage.com/poets/Stevenson/wha t_man_may_learn.html>, 10 Apr. 2002.

"Tabernacle Tombstones." <u>Pinckney District Chapter Newsletter</u>
<u>Vol. 10</u>. Spartanburg: <u>1989 SC Genealogical Society.</u> 1989.

<u>Walnut Grove Methodist Church, A History.</u> Eds. Rebekeh Gray,
Jackie McAbee and Rev. Janet Joens. Roebuck: Walnut
Grove Methodist Church 1996.

Westmoreland, Edna. Personal communication to Toya Harvey 26
Aug. 1993.

Willey, Basil. <u>Coleridge</u>. New York: W.W. Norton and Co., Inc.
1972.

My Family Fabric

A Story of the Allen, Rogers, Creighton,
League, Bruton, Gates, Smith Ancestors,
And My Immediate Harvey Family

I.S.B.N. 1-59879-085-4

Order Online at:
www.authorstobelievein.com

By Phone Toll Free at:
1-877-843-1007